SOUTHERN LITERARY STUDIES

FRED HOBSON, EDITOR

NOTES FROM THE

POST-MILLENNIAL SOUTH

gather

at the river

HAL CROWTHER

FOREWORD BY LOUIS D. RUBIN, JR.

LOUISIANA STATE UNIVERSITY PRESS
BATON ROUGE

DESIGNER: Barbara Neely Bourgoyne
TYPEFACE: Whitman; Helvetica Neue
PRINTER AND BINDER: Thomson-Shore, Inc.

LIBRARY OF CONGRESS CATALOGING-IN-PUBLICATION DATA:
Crowther, Hal.
  Gather at the river : notes from the post-millennial South / Hal Crowther ; foreword
by Louis D. Rubin, Jr.
    p. cm. — (Southern literary studies)
  ISBN 0-8071-3100-8 (alk. paper)
    1. American literature—Southern States—History and criticism. 2. Southern States—
Intellectual life. 3. Southern States—In literature. 4. Southern States—Civilization.
I. Title. II. Series.
PS261.C66 2005
810.9'975—dc22

                                                              2005005668

The author offers grateful acknowledgment to the editors of the *Oxford American*, the *New
York Times*, the *Independent Weekly*, *Southern Cultures*, the *Southeast Review*, *Menckeniana*,
and *Creative Loafing*, where these essays first appeared. Personal thanks to Fred Hobson,
Lee Smith, Mona Sinquefield, George Roupe, and John Grooms and especially to Louis D.
Rubin, Jr., without whose wisdom the literary South might yet be terra incognita.

For my mother,
Dorothy Louise Allen Crowther,
who is still discovering the South

Being of these hills
I cannot pass beyond.

—JAMES STILL

Hollywood says
Southerners are retarded,
but we sure can sing.

—BILL MALONE

Contents

Foreword

LOUIS D. RUBIN, JR.

Hal Crowther tells us that as a fourteen-year-old he went to sleep each night with an autographed baseball under his pillow and a copy of *The Vintage Mencken* close by. Clearly both exposures took. He writes literary and cultural commentary with a verve that makes most such seem pallid by comparison. And if asked he can invoke the names of major league outfielders and infielders long since fled to Cooperstown or elsewhere.

Make no mistake about it: as the essays in *Gather at the River* will illustrate, here is one of the ablest practitioners of the art of critical prose now at work. He has a way of knifing through cant and pomposity to expose what's truly at issue. Get him on a subject he knows something about—and he almost never writes about anything that he doesn't—and he swiftly distinguishes between what is authentic and what is hokum. No one I can think of does it better.

His recurrent though not sole focus in this book has to do in one way or another with the nature of things in the South. He opens in Asheville and, following numerous forays along the way, ends up in Baltimore. I daresay that if anyone can understand the place and its inhabitants these days, Crowther probably does. It's been a quarter century now since he came back for good, after graduation from Williams College and some years of journalism in New York City and elsewhere in the frozen northland. His is the kind of in-depth view that involves equal parts of familiarity and distancing. I can't believe that while majoring in English at Williams and covering sports for *Time* he would ever have anticipated how he would one day be caught up in the South, its customs, attitudes, and preoccupations. (So far as I know, however, he hasn't forsaken the Mets for the Atlanta Braves.)

I do not mean that Hal Crowther has become an apologist for the South. Good heavens, no! If he is an apologist for anything whatever, I have not discovered it. To the contrary, he is in no way reluctant to search out the regional iniquities, of which there are more than a few, with unerring acuteness and resonance. Read his comments on certain politicos, on racial attitudes, on the South's penchant for joyfully supporting any and all military interventions, on Dixie-style corporate slickness, on threadbare romanticism, tourist-trade opportunism, etc. The ongoing clinical report offered within these pages can be devastating, because he knows what he is talking about.

At the same time, what is guaranteed to draw his indignation is hauteur or condescension toward the South: what Robert Penn Warren described as the Northern "Treasury of Virtue." Having himself long since come to understand how very complex an entity the region is, he not only declines to countenance stereotypes and facile judgments from north of what was once referred to as the Smith & Wesson Line but is swift to nail the perpetrators.

To respond vigorously to sanctimonious moralizing from outside is a time-honored Southern custom. Crowther does not, however, stop there; he knows that the myopia of the critic does not necessarily invalidate the critique. Consider an excellent piece entitled "The Old Dragons Sleep," occasioned by the retirements of J. Strom Thurmond and Jesse Helms from the Senate of the United States. Upon the departure of the former, whose senatorial chair had been handed down from John C. Calhoun and Pitchfork Ben Tillman in a direct line of descent, there was a tearful farewell matinee in which Senator Trent Lott (R., Miss.) became so carried away that he suggested the nation would be better off today if only it had adhered to the social and constitutional assumptions of Thurmond's prime years: i.e., before *Brown v. Board of Education*. The ensuing tumult was ferocious, the upshot being that Lott was made to relinquish his post as majority leader in order to avoid being kicked out by his GOP colleagues.

Here is Crowther's response, or a portion of it:

> The quick clean castration of Senator Lott delighted Southern liberals, black and white; it gave punch-drunk Democrats a rare taste of blood that was not their own. But for the South there was no net gain in this ritual humiliation of a Mississippi mossback. In Manhattan, no one would have blinked if Lott's wardrobe had yielded a hooded Klan robe. They honestly believe that half of us have one hanging somewhere—not freshly pressed for a rally, necessarily, but at least in the back of the closet, where a man of fashion might hang his old white dinner jacket just in case.

Crowther's diagnosis is that what Trent Lott embodied in politics was something more cunning and calculating than the traditional stars-and-bars-brandishing, keep-the-white-race-pure Dixiecrat. "It was always a neat trick to feed the fires of racial resentment with one hand and wave the torch of equality with the other," he declares. "Change is dramatic in the modern South but very, very recent," and like many another agile politico in what these days is called the Sunbelt, Lott made it to the top because he knew how to continue to manipulate the region's hoary racial attitudes: "The old dragons are asleep now; for most of them it's a deep sleep, but never mistake it for death."

In another, more light-hearted commentary, he takes up a narrative by a young New Englander chronicling her travels into the remote provinces of the South—a phenomenon also not exactly without historical precedent. The author set out to interpret the South's psycho-history by taping folktale tellers and "running their tales through her personal software." Crowther is not impressed: "We are no Samoans; she's no Margaret Mead. She is, arguably, the most clue-less Outlander to write about the South since V. S. Naipaul's *A Turn in the South*. But she's no V. S. Naipaul, either."

Yet he takes care to credit her zeal. "Lost repeatedly, frustrated by maps and cloverleafs and traffic cops, betrayed by her tape recorder, this Ivy League intellectual turns out to be an endearing screwup," he decides, and he offers this delicately-phrased advice: "Never tell the South you understand it better than it understands itself. Like Brer Rabbit, it may outfox and outlast you."

A number of the essays in this book have to do with writing and writers, country and gospel music and musicians, painters, stage and screen productions, etc. These are among the best pieces, and I can only wish that more people could write about the arts of the South with as much perceptiveness and imagination. There is a first-rate piece on Thomas Wolfe, based on a visit to his mother's onetime boarding-house in Asheville, and another centered on Elizabeth Spencer, oc-casioned by her account of an evening spent with Eudora Welty and Katherine Anne Porter. Two provocative essays chronicle writers' conferences, one held in Key West, the other in Nashville. The first-named assemblage appears to have devolved into a declamatory brawl over whether immersion in geographical place or the workings of unencumbered literary imagination is of greater importance. As if an either/or choice were ever involved!

On the latter occasion, the goal was seemingly to arrive at a com-mon strategy for today's Southern writers and musicians to cope with a much-altered literary and cultural status quo. Crowther likens the attempt to "hitching up a team of panthers to pull a hay wagon." He insists that "every writer truly worth reading arrives with one essen-tial, a skewed, eccentric, arresting way of looking at the world—an oblique angle of vision that defies assimilation." Amen to that.

There is a delightful account of lunch during the Nashville con-clave with his novelist wife and Dolly Parton. "One of my litmus tests for Southern authenticity," he says, "would be the ability to appreciate the paradox of Dolly Parton: behind a blinding surface of deliberate, exaggerated, self-satirizing artifice lurks one of the most engagingly authentic individuals in the Nashville pantheon."

One could go on. I might cite, among assorted other choice items, his several forays into Southern music; his apt commentary on the decline and fall of the literary deconstructionists; his eloquent memoir of the reign of Kirk Varnedoe as curator of painting and sculpture at the Museum of Modern Art; or, my favorite of all, his description of the spiritual joys of Key West, where "I'm as far from home as I can go without a passport."

The finale in this collection is an essay on Mencken, originally prepared as the Mencken's Birthday address at the Enoch Pratt Library in Baltimore. Earlier he has remarked, "If memoir is a deep pool that's clogged with the corpses of the drowned, writers keep diving in anyway, like lemmings." But here he uses memories of his own family to help get at what made the Sage of Baltimore what he was and was not. Scoffing at Mencken's fancies about the vanished glories of an overrated aristocracy, whether of blood or learning, he sees him as the outcome of three generations of solid middle-class comfort and probity, producing an abiding conviction of freedom. "It takes a certain kind of family to incubate a critic, a columnist, a cynic, an iconoclast—someone with the serene self-confidence to assert in public that he is right and the herd, however vast or menacing, is not only wrong but ridiculous."

It seems to me, as a lifelong connoisseur of Mencken myself, that Crowther has a remarkably keen sense of the emotional and intellectual dynamics that propelled the Sage along his passionate way. And if there is any doubt about the continuing relevance of the old maxim that It takes one to call one, let me quote yet another sentence by Crowther. He is discussing the latter-day decline of that confidence in personal freedom that made an H. L. Mencken possible: "What I see now is a victorious plutocracy, mind-altering marketing technology delivered into its grateful hands like a genie in a magic lamp, purging its captive population of any lingering idealism or self-respect that might get in the way of perfect, seamless, thoughtless consumption."

Appropriately titled "Mencken and Me: Indiscreet Charms of the Bourgeoisie," the essay concludes as vigorous and adventuresome a set of pieces, mostly about the South, as anyone with a taste for good sense and sharp insights set forth in lustrous prose might ask. I don't agree with all of Crowther's opinions—only about 95 percent of them. I think he can overdo the apocalyptic note. But there's not a plodding sentence or an inane comment in *Gather at the River*, and I envy any reader about to encounter him for the first time.

gather at the river

The Tao of Dixie

A STUBBORN PEOPLE

A foreigner from Scotland or California will visit a large Southern city—usually Atlanta—and complain that he could never find the South of song and story. Just another Minneapolis, as far as he could see, with the heat turned up and a few magnolias. Maybe our visitor stayed at the Ritz Carlton, where businessmen parting company at the bar say, "Hit 'em straight, fella," instead of "My best to June and the kids." He was never invited to the Piedmont Driving Club and never ventured more than a few miles from Buckhead.

Nevertheless he has a point. The vital, urban South, where unemployment is low and ringworm unheard of, has long since built museums for its myths and moved on. Even in the unimproved countryside, where kudzu still creeps and gnats still swarm among the pecan trees, a visitor listens long and hard to catch the faintest echo of Margaret Mitchell or Erskine Caldwell either. Assimilation, once the great fear, is now the great fact of most Southern lives.

Why, then, are libraries bursting with dissertations on the metaphysics of Southernness, why are panels convened, sages summoned, centers dedicated to study the Tao of Dixie? Why is Southern separateness—among the reflective class no less than the belligerent—an enduring strain of separateness no other American region can approach or comprehend?

These are questions people ask me, more often since I published a book subtitled *A Personal Landscape of the South*. Radio personalities have trapped me and compelled me to answer. Sometimes the pitiless microphone betrays my hesitation, my confusion. And then there are moments when it all seems crystal clear.

There's a musical entertainment called *Good Ol' Girls*, a collaboration between novelists Lee Smith and Jill McCorkle and Nashville songwriters Matraca Berg and Marshall Chapman. It's a show for seven women, who sing and play various female characters from the fiction of Smith and McCorkle. *Girls* is a revue with an attitude, one I characterized inadequately as redneck feminism. In spite of its burden of intelligence, it played to raucous sellout crowds in North Carolina and Virginia and attracted the attention of a New York producer.

Mr. Big took the whole cast to Manhattan for what's called a show-case production, to seduce investors for a run in an off-Broadway theater. The "Girls" gave one of their best performances for an audience that included many of the New York theater's prominent rainmakers. Several days later the producer called in director/adapter Paul Ferguson and gave him Broadway's verdict: Nice try, nice music, but not half "Southern" enough. The women were too pretty, too smart, too normal, too middle-class. And all those words between the songs? The Broadway big shots offered their own version of *Good Ol' Girls*—three or four grits-eating grannies with big hair, bad teeth and banjoes.

New York's idea of a good old girl is Mammy Yokum. Since the whole point of the show was to exterminate *Hee Haw* stereotypes of Southern women, the collaborators were amazed and appalled. They faced a limited menu of conclusions about the creative geniuses who dominate the New York theater: Are they low-grade morons with the cultural IQs of root vegetables, cynical mercenaries who operate on the threshold of pure evil, or uncritical consumers of Southern stereotypes that haven't been updated since the Second World War?

From that menu my responses are (1) "possibly" (2) "very likely," and (3) "definitely." The South has changed rapidly, but it doesn't take many trips to New York to convince you that its image has not.

Faulkner's Gavin Stevens complains that Northerners suffer from "a gullibility, a volitionless, almost helpless capacity and eagerness to believe anything about the South not even provided it be derogatory but merely bizarre enough and strange enough."

"Fundamentalism, Ku Kluxry, revivals, lynchings, hog wallow politics—these are the things that always occur to a Northerner when he thinks of the South," wrote H. L. Mencken, whose disparaging satires helped keep the South in its unenviable place. What little Mencken left untarnished was soiled forever by the Broadway production of Erskine Caldwell's *Tobacco Road*, which logged a record 3,180 performances during the Great Depression.

"What sets Southerners apart?" asks *Time* magazine in a 1964 cover story. Its first hypothesis, courtesy of Caldwell's Jeeter Lester: "Is poverty too prevalent? Is sex too obsessive?"

This nagging Yankee suspicion that the sex is hotter somewhere else—Harlem, Paris, Latin America, Savannah—has been a curse for the sons of the Puritans since the days of Jonathan Edwards. But 7 million Americans saw *Tobacco Road*, and the South has never recovered from Caldwell's sordid caricatures. The play closed in 1941; *Time* proved that New York's mind was still closed in 1964, and *Good Ol' Girls* proved that it hasn't opened much in the past half century.

Why search any further to account for the South's stubborn tribal attitude, its adamant embrace of a separate identity even as the floodwaters of mass culture wash away its monuments and shrines? Tribal consciousness—the chip on the shoulder underdogs wear as a fraternal badge—persists as long as the tribe suffers misrepresentation, misunderstanding, prejudice and contempt. The "pride" of these pride marches—gay, black, feminist—is nothing more than defiance, the beleaguered defiance of tribes who feel excluded, slandered, and oppressed.

Bigotry, which never varies, measures a whole tribe by its most offensive and ridiculous representatives. If we accept witless stereotypes as the common coin of oppression, what group has a more legitimate grievance than Southerners? In a prescient speech titled "The Idea of the South," delivered in Houston in 1963, North Carolina historian George B. Tindall traced the pedigree of our toxic mythology—from Caldwell and Mencken back to Harriet Beecher Stowe and A. B. Longstreet—and quoted what must be the classic lament of the Southerner misunderstood:

> "Even today the Northern visitor hankers to see eroded hills and rednecks, scrub cotton and sharecropper shacks," John T. Westbrook of Louisiana wrote in 1960. " . . . The fumes of progress are in his nose and the bright steel of industry towers before his eyes, but his heart is away in Yoknapatawpha county with razorback hogs and night riders. . . . He wants, above all else, to sniff the effluvium of backwoods-and-sandhill subhumanity and to see at least one barn burn at midnight. So he looks at me with crafty misgivings, as if to say, 'Well, you do talk rather glibly about Kierkegaard and Sartre . . . but after all, you're only fooling, aren't you? Don't you, sometimes, go out secretly by owl-light to drink swampwater and feed on sowbelly and collard greens?'"

Northerners are so besotted with these myths, Professor Tindall suggested, they take Faulkner for a realist.

As long as popular culture persists in presenting them as incestuous hillbillies, church-burners, mule-beaters and randy evangelists, Southerners will dip snuff and fly Confederate battle flags just to make New Yorkers wince. This unlikely mixture of defiant pride and self-mockery is a joke Northern liberals never grasp. I think it helps to explain why North Carolina kept Jesse Helms in the U.S. Senate for thirty years. He's a monstrous mascot, a gross pet we harbored in the same spirit as people who keep pythons and ferrets. Tar Heels reelected him as long as he was capable of throwing the Eastern media into apoplexy.

Irony is a secret pleasure, an idiom that eludes the media and tends to multiply misunderstandings. Sly and impertinent, the South has preserved its self-respect at the expense of its public relations.

But this cultural impasse was a serious handicap for Jimmy Carter and Bill Clinton, two of the most intelligent and able men elected president in the twentieth century. The media and the Washington establishment—talk about incest—saw Carter and Clinton through a distorting lens of cornpone stereotype: Carter the peanut farmer, a sort of guileless Sunday school Baptist in starched overalls; Clinton the leering fornicator, at best a dirt-roads drummer with an itch for farm girls, at worst Jeeter Lester with a Yale education.

Are we paranoid? I don't think so. A few weeks ago I was trying to convince a friend, a brilliant, benevolent scholar from the Northeast, that sympathy for defenders of the Confederate battle flag was not beyond all rational consideration.

"Would you let them fly the Nazi flag?" he replied, and my jaw dropped a foot and a half.

It's that kind of insensitivity that keeps the South resentful, obstinate, a little xenophobic, and best of all distinct. It brings out the Rebel even in mild mongrel Southerners like me. Among blooded, old-growth Confederates it brings out the emotional equivalent of Pickett's Charge.

In 1956 a British reporter famously quoted William Faulkner: "If it came to fighting I'd fight for Mississippi against the United States even if it meant going out into the street and shooting Negroes." Of course this was recorded out of context while the author was adrift on a two-day drunk. In the same interview he repeatedly said "The Negroes are right" and the white racists "wrong, and their position untenable." It wasn't Faulkner's politics but his fierce, beleaguered tribal spirit the Englishman captured, the spirit that wrote (of Chick Mallison, hero of *Intruder in the Dust*): "He wanted no more save to stand with them unalterable and impregnable: one shame if shame must be, one expiation must surely be but above all one unalterable durable impregnable one: one people one heart one land."

He wasn't just whistling Dixie.

I. Words and Music

BUT WE SURE CAN SING

The Word

The Shoes of a Giant

On a curb that flanks the parking lot of the Renaissance Hotel in Asheville, North Carolina, the unwitting tourist confronts an enormous pair of tortured-looking shoes. At first glance they look like something cast off by a derelict reduced to negotiating the mean streets of downtown Asheville in his stocking feet. But something about the orderly way they sit there—as if a bellman might come out and pick them up for a shine—invites a closer inspection. Looming just behind the shoes is the Thomas Wolfe Memorial, the twenty-nine-room "Old Kentucky Home" ("Dixieland" in *Look Homeward, Angel*) where Wolfe grew up among his mother's boarders. Gutted by fire and closed to visitors for several years, the monstrous old house was being reconstructed, slowly, under blankets of blue rainproof plastic.

There's no obvious connection between the shoes and the Wolfe Memorial. But what I discovered on the curb was a literary relic, an actual pair of Wolfe's gargantuan shoes, lovingly bronzed by a local garden club and set in a memorial plaque that jests predictably about how hard it would be to fill these shoes.

Like ten thousand fools before me, I stepped up next to the big shoes and made the inevitable comparison. My black Reeboks are size twelves; the Asheville Giant appears to have me by at least four sizes, never mind the width.

Thomas Wolfe was a great big man, nearly six and a half feet tall in his stocking feet. His awesome shoes were custom made, like his coffin, and when he died he owned a literary reputation to match. For better than half a century, scholars with little picks and chisels have chipped away at the towering reputation that once cast its shadow, like Mount Mitchell, over all the lesser peaks and tamer ranges of Southern letters. In 2000, the centennial year of his birth, Wolfe's stock was so deflated that his fierce partisans—of whom there are many—were struggling just to hold his place on the exotic fringe of the canon.

What have they done with Thomas Wolfe, to whom William Faulkner once ceded first place among all American writers of the twenties and thirties? (Faulkner ranked himself second.) To my surprise the question seemed important again, after one night in a seventh-floor hotel room with a bird's-eye view of Wolfe's bronze shoes and his mother's dreadful house. As if some revenant with a grievance had whispered in my ear while I slept.

Wolfe's was no ordinary spirit; Asheville is no ordinary place. Driving north from Asheville on the remarkable Blue Ridge Parkway, you climb straight into the clouds. In a few minutes you're a mile above sea level, and the Great Smoky Mountains spread out below and around you in a panoramic extravagance beyond anything east of the Rockies, as vast and blue and breathtaking as anything on this continent. I pull over at the first high overlook on the parkway, where a marker reads: "The last buffalo seen in this locality was killed nearby in 1799 by Joseph Rice, an early settler."

I'm still being haunted by comparisons. Wolfe wouldn't have shared my trite, eco-sentimental sigh for the last Eastern bison and the biodiversity lost because our ancestors' one approach to wildlife management was ballistic. He'd have eyes only for the sublime, for the alpine valleys and range after range of blue mountains beyond. Then I remember, from researching a magazine article a few years ago, that Wolfe hated the mountains.

Scholar John Idol, writing in *Appalachian Journal,* made an impressive attempt to reclaim Asheville's wayward giant for Appalachian literature, citing later works like *The Hills Beyond* where Wolfe is less ambivalent, at times even sentimental about the hills of home. But for most game that dog won't hunt. Wolfe's agent, Elizabeth Nowell, recalled that he had no use for nature and never learned the names of "the commonest birds or trees or flowers." By choice he lived most of his adult life in New York City. He was a more familiar figure in Paris than in North Carolina.

Maxwell Perkins, who edited *Look Homeward, Angel,* spoke of Asheville's mountains "imprisoning" Wolfe's imagination.

"The mountains hem you in and hold you and never let you go," complains a character in one of Wolfe's first plays.

The late James Still, the Kentucky Methuselah who was Thomas Wolfe's last living contemporary among Southern writers, chose similar words to express a very different emotion. "I shall not leave these prisoning hills," begins Still's poem "Heritage," which hangs framed in the kitchen of our house near the Blue Ridge Parkway in Ashe County, North Carolina. "Being of these hills I cannot pass beyond."

Wolfe's difference, of course, is that he mistook his feelings for mountains—for Everest, Chimborazo, Denali, Popocatepetl—and among them he found the crags and precipices, the coves and waterfalls that were for him a source of endless fascination. A colossus of self-reference, he was the intrepid explorer of the Andes and Himalayas of himself. In one of his lectures he described himself as spewing forth material "like masses of lava from a volcano." Enthroned on his inner Olympus, he didn't need to climb Mount Mitchell to feel like a god.

Like that last poor bison, Thomas Wolfe's an easy target—high, wide and woolly and too big to miss, in the flesh or on the printed page. He's not hard to understand or deconstruct: if he didn't actually write down every thought he ever had, he came close enough to leave us the simulacrum of an unbroken stream of consciousness.

Many writers have felt superior to Wolfe, cooler and more controlled, better at driving a large idea around a banked track without running into the wall. Most people who write about Wolfe have lived to be older than he ever was, and we all know things he never learned. How old were you when you last felt like a Eugene—or Eugenia—Gant? When you imagined that all the world's pain and all its majesty was assembled out there just to backlight your journey and sing harmony for the epic song of your soul?

"He wanted opulent solitude," Wolfe wrote of Gant. "His dark vision burned on kingdoms under the sea, on windy castle crags and on the deep elf kingdoms at the earth's core. . . ."

Ego alone won't sustain such flights. They require innocence, too. Wolfe died young, not quite thirty-eight. He was emotionally arrested, a big brilliant dream-addled child. *Look Homeward, Angel* and *Of Time and the River* are views from the starting gate, almost before "real" life commences. But so are *Huckleberry Finn* and *The Magic Mountain.*

His innocence is as unfashionable as his effusion, and his grandiloquence. Yet many of the critics who condescend to Wolfe are not his equals. This was no literary ruffian but an erudite giant who devoured Western literature with the same appetite he brought to sex and fried chicken.

"He spoke well, had read everything, knew everything." recalled the late Cleanth Brooks, who was present in Richmond in 1936 when Wolfe, gripping a bottle of whiskey, delivered an unscheduled lecture on poetry to Robert Penn Warren and the MLA.

Wolfe for all his awkward sprawl was not a primitive. He was an anachronism, a throwback to the turn of an earlier century, to those German and English Romantics he all but memorized. As a people, Americans don't think like Wolfe anymore. They're hive creatures who network and conform, and practice petty avarice and sell themselves cheap. Self-absorption is epidemic but it's expended in therapy and self-pity, scarcely ever in the Promethean struggle that consumed Thomas Wolfe.

When I think of Wolfe, I think of a tragic scene from the annals of vertebrate evolution: a huge, ungainly bird, aerodynamically unsound, ill-designed for flight but straining—eyes wild, beak open wide, heavy wings creaking—to clear the last ridge and soar. Feathers are falling. What stuns us is not the height or length of the flight, but the stupendous effort, the aspiration—a metaphor, like the myth of Icarus, for the human soul and the human condition.

Wolfe, never quite a great writer or a great intellect, was a great creative force field—a consciousness charged with uncommon grandeur. Too many of us are blessed or cursed with irony, the best antidote for the hubris that challenges the gods. Irony is symbiotic with humility. But if everyone felt dwarfed by existential insights, who'd produce great works of art, or even great feats of engineering like the Blue Ridge Parkway, Appalachia's bold answer to the Great Wall of China?

Irony never grounded Thomas Wolfe, never diluted what Elizabeth Hardwick calls his "assertion of primordial selfhood." Addressing a freshman assembly at the University of North Carolina, the sixteen-year-old Wolfe announced that his portrait would one day hang on that wall next to ex-presidents and Confederate generals (it does).

For a few people egomania is more than a weakness for pleasing themselves at the expense of others. It's a physical deformity, a gross fact like the one that confronted Wolfe every morning when he looked down and thought, "Those are damn big feet I have there."

Individuals with bloated, disfiguring egos often drink themselves to death or become dictators or ruthless tycoons. Wolfe did much better. He left this record, these massive documents marbled with prose poems that still inspire and intoxicate, to attest to a life that drab mortals can barely imagine. He left great alarming footprints—like the Sasquatch—and defied the puny ironist to fill his shoes.

Landmarks

THE THREE GRACES

In Elizabeth Spencer's short story "A Southern Landscape," an enormous antebellum ruin called Windsor is locally famous—in fictional Port Claiborne, Mississippi—because its cupola was once so high you could see it from the river, and pilot Mark Twain was reputed to have steered by it. The narrator, Marilee, a practical girl, notes in characteristic fashion that she has read *Life on the Mississippi* and that in fact Twain steered by nearly anything: "crawfish mounds, old rowboats stuck in the mud, the tassels on somebody's corn patch, and every stump and stob from New Orleans to Cairo, Illinois."

To many who have never made the journey, Southern literature is like its big river—over-traveled and over-observed, and steered by landmarks of little consequence to anyone but the natives. It's true that no place on earth celebrates or scrutinizes its writers as the South has; it's probably true that literary chauvinism and self-consciousness were accelerated by H. L. Mencken's notorious attacks on Southern culture in the 1920s. But the great Renaissance, the one that seemed to spring from Mencken's contempt, was real. My advice to a contemporary student of Southern literature is to take a rain check on the cutting-edge crowd and also on the critics, traditional or revisionist. Go back on up the river—a river of time, in this case—and take the whole trip from Cairo to the Vieux Carré.

A few of time's landmarks loom as high as Windsor's cupola, and every pilot has his favorites. One of mine is a summer evening in Pass Christian, Mississippi, in 1951, in a high-ceilinged room in the old Miramar Hotel. This is a scene from a film, though no cameras were present. The young woman in the chair is Eudora Welty, the older woman in the bed, propped up on pillows, feeling poorly, is Katherine Anne Porter. The youngest woman, sitting on the floor, is Elizabeth Spencer.

Three women literally worth a thousand stories, a whole literary tradition talking quietly in a hotel room on the Gulf Coast. It was a summer of the Korean War, of Cold War hysteria and spies—Julius and Ethel Rosenberg had just been convicted, Guy Burgess and Donald Maclean had just fled London for Moscow. J. D. Salinger had just published *The Catcher in the Rye*. The previous December, William Faulkner had received his Nobel Prize in Stockholm and made his famous speech—"I believe that man will not merely endure: he will prevail"—against the pervasive fear that seemed to be enveloping the world.

There's only one living witness to the meeting at the Miramar, and with typical self-effacement Spencer, in her memoir *Landscapes of the Heart*, remembers herself listening to the older women talk. "Katherine Anne was lying on the bed recounting her experiences—such experiences," Spencer told me, "and Eudora and I were her audience." But when I implied that hers was the role of the little sister in this company, Spencer pushed that away. "Katherine Anne may have seen me that way. I didn't know her. But Eudora never treated me like a little sister or a protégée, not from the moment we met. We were always friends and equals. That's the way Eudora was, the only way she'd have it."

I asked her to describe Katherine Anne Porter. Porter, who died in 1980, may be the only writer, male or female, whose "countless other painful love affairs" are part of the standard bio in academic anthologies. I used the phrase "body language," which made Spencer laugh.

"To comment on her body language you'd have to be male," she said, her voice going high as it does when she's amused. "She was impressive to look at, more than a little attractive. She told us, 'I would have been able to do much more, except for the many interruptions—by that I mean the time I've given to men.'"

One remarkable thing about the three women at the Miramar is the size of their achievement—read the collected stories of all three and you've earned a master's degree in Deep South studies without ever consulting a man. And another is their curious failure to match any of the venerable stereotypes of the Southern woman, least of all the ones they manipulate in their fiction.

Porter, my grandmother's age, was an unsinkable farmer's daughter from East Texas who used her way with words and men to range the world and forge a one-of-a-kind reputation. Sometime actress, artist, and revolutionary, full-time scandal, Porter set many of her stories in genteel Christian parlors where she would not have been welcome. Eudora Welty, a generation younger, relished her freedom as a special case in a closed society where every woman, married or unmarried, was supposed to be dependent on her family. Welty's image in old age, receiving worshipful pilgrims at her house in Jackson, bears little resemblance to the intrepid traveler and continental sophisticate we encounter in memoirs like Spencer's. Welty wrote about home, but she was never a stay-at-home until time clipped her wings.

Spencer, a child in the Jazz Age South of flappers and rumble seats, faced fewer obstacles to liberation and an artist's vocation. But she found too many in Clarksdale, Mississippi, where she was related to everyone. A Guggenheim took her to Italy and the literary life, and in Rome she met an Englishman from Cornwall, John Rusher. After their marriage they lived in Montreal for thirty years, and moved to Chapel Hill in 1986. Spencer never got more than halfway home to Mississippi.

None of these ladies led a sheltered or even a cautious life, and it's not surprising that the conversation in Pass Christian touched on men as much as books. Spencer, reticent about the specifics, recalls the tone as ironic but not unkind. I've observed firsthand how

Welty and Spencer enjoyed the company of younger men. They both inspired extremes of protective chivalry. You could easily look up Spencer's age, for instance, but you couldn't get it out of me with thumbscrews. Welty with her perfect courtesy was the wise aunt, the older sister who saw and understood all male, indeed all human frailty and forgave it.

Elizabeth Spencer is a shy woman with a natural reserve she can lower, when it's called for, like a set of Venetian blinds. But like the Southern belles she disparages, she seems practiced in the detection and management of testosterone. My wife once described her "Sphinx-like, almost seductive smile." I don't know that I've ever seen Elizabeth more animated, or more charming, than the night of James Dickey's wake in Columbia, when the sad part was over and the bourbon came out and she found herself at a table for six with five admiring men.

An amusing aspect of the generation gap is the way our children choose to discount our sins and passions, how they refuse to acknowledge that we were ever young. It's funnier to me now that I'm on the elderly side of this misunderstanding—the coals are still smoldering from the hell we raised, and the next generation thinks we're huddled by the fire to keep warm. These children might be astonished by the fiction of Elizabeth Spencer, which I imagine them dismissing, in their ignorance, as restrained and tepid lady literature. In fact it's full of reckless drinking, creative sin and sexual misbehavior. In her short story "The Business Venture," we find compulsive adultery within a clique of archetypal small-town swingers; in *Ship Island*, lethal male creatures, as repellent as Popeye in Faulkner's *Sanctuary*, lie in wait for the girl who's looking for trouble. In her novel *The Snare*, a beguiling old pervert waits in an airless upstairs room in New Orleans.

As a writer, Spencer has never been afraid to open the door to the darkness. Nothing human is censored. The difference between a Spencer story and a slice of *Rough South* from Harry Crews or Larry Brown lies in the social class of the characters, mainly, and in the language she chooses to describe their sins. Though I used to pester editors to let me use four-letter words, now I find it irresistible when

Spencer, in her memoir, describes a homosexual as "not the kind, as they said in those days, to have girl friends." Faulkner's mistress, Joan Williams, is introduced as "a special interest of William Faulkner's."

"I don't know if I'm shockable by language," she told me. "I like Barry Hannah, and he's pretty rough. But there's a difference between facing up to ugly things and wallowing in them."

What most of her protagonists hold in common is an unfocused but overpowering longing. "The constant subject of Spencer's fiction is passion," wrote Lee Smith. There's always a pulse in it, and there was a strong pulse, always, in the woman who wrote it. "I think back on the many ways of falling in love," she writes in *Landscapes*, "a good number of which I can report on firsthand. . ." On the page preceding her account of the evening at the Miramar, she reminisces about burning a tall stack of love letters in the back yard. "The smoke was at least good for keeping the mosquitoes off," she recalls, in a voice like Marilee's.

Of the distinguished trinity who convened at the Miramar, Porter and Welty achieved their greatest public success—bestsellers, films, Pulitzer Prizes—late in life. Spencer reached hers early, in 1960, when her novella *The Light in the Piazza* was a commercial and critical triumph and a major motion picture with Olivia De Havilland and Rossano Brazzi. During the years in Montreal, she was a larger figure in Canadian and world literature than in the closely guarded canon of her native South. That changed with her return. Much has changed: Spencer is a widow now, and Welty, her friend of fifty years, is gone, too. The Miramar and most of her beloved Gulf Coast landmarks were destroyed by Hurricane Camille in 1969. But she's learning, as Porter and Welty learned before her, that if you live long enough your career will grow new chapters, addenda, footnotes, epilogues. Spencer's most recent collection, *The Southern Woman* (2001) will be published in paperback in the fall. In June she flew to Seattle for the premiere of a new musical based on *The Light in the Piazza*, with songs by Richard Rodgers's grandson, Adam Guettel. It was a hit in Chicago and opened in New York in April, to rave reviews.

"My books are all in print, all but one," Spencer told me. "And there are so many encouraging people here in North Carolina. I really can't complain." And very conspicuously she doesn't. If you read *Landscapes of the Heart*, you won't find a word about aging. Published in 1998, it ends with a new beginning—leaving Canada—and promises the reader "a whole new volume" when she finds the time.

First Person Singular

A BOY AND HIS DOG

Last week a rambling dinner conversation turned to the gross excesses of the flourishing memoir industry. The worst thing I could document was a reading at the PEN-Faulkner dinner in Washington by the noted incest author Katharine Harrison, whose work in progress included a graphic reminiscence of eating her grandmother's ashes. There was an unconfirmed report that Hillary Clinton rose from her seat, at the mastication of the cremated remains, and sought sanctuary in the ladies' room.

Novelist Ann Beattie topped me immediately, citing a memoir by a poet who confessed to an extended sexual relationship with the family dog, an unfortunate and—worse—unwilling creature named Fluffy. The poet, she said, now regrets publishing this memoir outré of his adolescence—not because he has a bad conscience but because the story hounds him, so to speak, and compromises his dignity. ("Lay one brick and it doesn't make you a bricklayer, but f—— one dog . . .")

These days a poet does what he can to attract a publisher's attention. Here at the millennium, memoir owes more to the influence of Jerry Springer than to the great American tradition of Twain, Thoreau, and Henry Adams. Intimate memoirs have become a lucrative literary striptease, a naughty chorus line of exhibitionists playing to an eager audience of voyeurs. Hacks and fools take their turn on the runway, flash their candy, pout at the sailors, and who really cares? But it hurts to look up and see one of your favorite writers wearing nothing but a feather boa.

There's a book that bothered me and still bothers me. I can't make my peace with it. Over the years, I've professed so much admiration for the fiction of Lewis Nordan that his publicist sends me his newsletter; when I read the working title of his memoir-in-progress, I spit up half a cup of coffee in my mirth. Who can top "Don't Cry for Me, Itta Bena"? But according to Nordan's publisher, Algonquin Books of Chapel Hill, the title tested as a Mississippi in-joke. In North Carolina and New York, no one knew how to pronounce Itta Bena. A bad omen. The memoir was published this winter as *Boy with Loaded Gun,* and it turned out to be a serious mistake.

Not everyone will agree with me. I hesitate to blame Algonquin, because for all I know *Boy* is the one book Nordan always wanted to write. But anyone with the good taste to publish a writer like Lewis Nordan ought to have the good sense to tell him when there's something he shouldn't publish.

Nordan, the author of *Wolf Whistle, Sharpshooter Blues,* and *Music of the Swamp,* is an amiable, unassuming man whose fiction issues from a huge heart and a pricelessly warped imagination. In a story like "The Wheelchair," there's this infinitely subtle pulse of pain and need and loss, a pure unfiltered compassion beyond most writers' grasp. As the benevolent proprietor of the dream-crossed Delta backwater of Arrow Catcher, Mississippi, Nordan owns an enviable literary persona.

Readers, even those who know better, like to imagine a favored writer as a kind of magus, one who understands the mysteries. This is a valuable illusion. Much magic is lost when the wizard stumbles from behind the screen in his dirty underwear, drunk and crying. What drove Nordan, in this memoir, to reveal things about himself that cautious people hide from their psychiatrists? It isn't that he tells us too much, exactly, but that he gives no sign that he understands his own material—his own life's trajectory.

How does a reader respond when the writer creates a hapless, damaged character, barely afloat and apparently without a clue, and confirms "Yes, this is me, my life has been hell, please give me a hug"? It's disarming, but is it literature? At times it reads more like an addict bearing witness at an AA meeting, which is also a part of Nordan's story.

There's no shame in failing to solve life's riddles or even to understand them. It's the bedrock human condition. But where memoir aspires to literature, where it tries to rise above journal entries and a chronology of anecdotes, the convention is to show wisdom gained, patterns perceived, obsessive and self-destructive behavior overcome. If the writer's actual life doesn't measure up to all this insight, no matter. Memoir, like fiction, succeeds by suggesting some symmetry, some comprehensible order lurking beneath the wreckage of human lives.

Among certain Southern writers there's been a kind of competition to determine who was raised roughest of all. But even these memoirs of being reared in the hogpen, slopped infrequently, and taken out only to be whipped and raped—even these stories of unspeakable white-trash wretchedness share the satisfaction of survivors who became viable adults. They share the convention that any life worth examining can teach us something.

George Garrett used to say that it was literature if it bore "news of the spirit." If *Boy with Loaded Gun* bears news of the spirit, it's bad news only. I didn't think Nordan could write a book that wasn't funny, yet he's managed it, almost. Weirdness has a charm in fiction that palls quickly in autobiography. A fictional character's tragicomic misadventures become serious as death when the writer claims them for his own and tells you how much they hurt.

The sex is especially painful. Writers' sexual confessions generally fall into two categories, the same old stuff—big yawn—and stuff they should have kept to themselves. Nordan's are *not* the same old stuff, unless your sex life also included group sex in a group that included a machine. There's one for the church ladies. But church ladies buy books. Isn't this akin to mooning the poor dears and driving them screaming from the house of letters?

Mostly it's sad. The reader's response is to feel sorry for the author, which oddly enough seems to be the author's intention. I confess I don't understand these extremes of autobiographical impulse. The raw-meat memoir may be the fashionable genre for a coarse, vicarious culture, but a little reticence makes the best appeal to the kind of reader a good writer hopes to reach. In autobiography or fiction, sex acts are more distracting than illuminating; your sexual abuse of Fluffy proves nothing except that you were a strange child to do it and a strange adult to publish it.

I hate to pick on Buddy Nordan, but I feel that he was misled. I know I'm a better friend to Nordan and his books than anyone who might have encouraged him to publish *Boy with Loaded Gun*. If you want to appreciate one of the South's most original writers, it's a book to avoid. If the art of the memoir is your interest, it's your textbook. By diving in blind and wounding himself, Nordan teaches us more about the parameters and pitfalls of the genre than a dozen elegant models like Eudora Welty's *One Writer's Beginnings* or William Alexander Percy's ostracized but fascinating *Lanterns on the Levee*.

In *Inventing the Truth* (Houghton Mifflin, 1987)—one of the few serious studies of the memoir—William Zinsser asserts that "the writer of a memoir must become the editor of his own life." It's not a role everyone can manage. Raw material is the one democratic thing in literature. Each of us lives a life that some writer could turn into a book of great wisdom and beauty. But it's funny how seldom that perfect master of your material is *you*.

For the wrong writer, the wrong candidate, the memoir is the most treacherous form of all. It's like the new bar girl you discover in the worst place in town: she looks easy and she makes you feel important, but she could end up with your wallet and you could end up on an IV.

If memoir is a deep pool that's clogged with the corpses of the drowned, writers keep diving in anyway, like lemmings. Many of my friends and half my favorite writers have attempted memoirs, and my wife is across the hall typing up something autobiographical. It's a modern epidemic of self-exposure.

That impulse to bare it all is usually the wrong impulse, the devil whispering. If you write fiction or poetry, a book-length memoir squanders ten years of material. Whatever you write, those stories you tell on yourself will stay in circulation, somewhere. Nordan's seduction, like poor Fluffy's, is now in the public domain, irretrievable. No one will believe him if he says he lied.

But these warnings fall on deaf ears. Agents and editors, whose most certain skill is understanding authors' egos, continue to lure their writers into this skin game of instant gratification and diminishing returns.

"*Ego,*" wrote William L. Shirer *(Rise and Fall of the Third Reich),* "is at the heart of all the reasons why anybody writes a memoir, whether it's a book or a pamphlet or a letter to our children. Memoir is how we validate our lives."

Most writers, God bless them, are natural egoists and exhibitionists—moths to the flame of memoir. And blind to the fate of an indiscreet poet who still gets an occasional elbow in the ribs at a cocktail party, and a smirking old friend barking "Woof! Woof!" in his ear.

Oral Misery

THE COLUMBUS SYNDROME

Americans never turn sentimental about something of real value—wilderness, wild animals, small towns, baseball, mountain music, our privacy—until the way we live and do business has pressed it to the edge of extinction. Then we administer affectionate last rites to everything we failed to love enough. In a culture where young and old feed their hunger for narrative from the electronic trash heap of television, it's hard to imagine a human resource more precious or endangered than America's storytellers, legitimate heirs to an oral tradition that was ancient when history was born. It's hard to withhold applause from a book that takes up the lost cause and the soon-to-be-lost art of folktales.

Hard, but not impossible. Pamela Petro's *Sitting Up with the Dead: A Storied Journey through the American South* is an odd book that strays from the marked trail of its author's best intentions and lures her, like many a folktale protagonist, into a dark swamp where the light she takes for insight may be nothing but fox fire.

Petro takes her first misstep when she decides that the stories she covets are inseparable from the identity and the history of the South. It may be true that the Southern states can claim the best surviving storytellers, or the most. But it was a mischievous voice that told Petro she could decipher the South—assuming it's a puzzle—by taping storytellers and running their tales through her personal software. (This journey into "the deep past," as she styles it, is rife with incongruous references to modems, e-mail, and the Internet.)

The South was never such an easy study, never such a seamless entity. Our problem with this book is what I call the Columbus syndrome. Indians were not amused by the notion that Columbus discovered America. The South is not amused to be rediscovered by Pamela Petro, intrepid explorer, cultural missionary to Darkest Dixie.

We are no Samoans; she's no Margaret Mead. She is, arguably, the most clueless Outlander to write about the South since V. S. Naipaul's *A Turn in the South*. But she's no V. S. Naipaul either.

This is, after all, a Rhode Island Yankee who had never heard of a pimento cheese sandwich or a hush puppy, who includes a long footnote to explain that mountaineers rarely mean "shout" when they say "holler." Candid to a fault, she admits that her abiding images of the South were dominated by bleeding civil rights marchers and snarling police dogs and that "Mississippi" is a word that chills her blood. At her most charmingly naïve, Petro confesses that her private code for the menacing Southland was the phrase "down there." To my late mother-in-law, a native of Tidewater Virginia, "down there" was a genteel euphemism for a woman's private parts.

But *Sitting Up with the Dead* was not aimed at the Southern reader. Since no Southern reviewer will praise it, I should note some virtues that foreign readers might appreciate. Petro is a fluent writer with considerable powers of description. In her best passages, she responds poetically to spooky or awe-inspiring landscapes that a native might take for granted. Her physical descriptions of the motley tribe of storytellers are deft, often droll. But as she says, "a few hundred pages don't have nearly as much personality as living, cussing, dancing, spitting, smoking, eating, drinking human beings."

Stories from the oral tradition need to be heard to be appreciated. Storytellers like North Carolina's seven-foot Ray Hicks need to be seen to be believed. Even a qualified native folklorist—they abound on Southern campuses—might have rated this project unpromising. When Petro embraced the genre of the personal quest, like Peter Matthiessen on the trail of the snow leopard or Carlos Castaneda in search of Don Juan, she assumed an added burden of credibility. Is this a life-altering obsession or just a book contract? I'd assign her pilgrimage more existential weight if I didn't know, from her acknowledgments, that it was suggested by friends at a party in 1998.

Petro's rental-car odyssey covered twelve states and several thousand miles of interstates and blue highways, more of the South on a tighter schedule than any motivated Yankee since General Sherman. But though she passed within a mile of my house and quotes several of my friends—though a prized pencil portrait of the giant Ray Hicks hangs over the table in our kitchen—there was no point in this book where I felt that Pamela Petro and I were on the same page. Page 348, where she deduces the Mind of the South from the ravings of Tennessee's Bell Witch, is a display of almost criminal opacity.

Still, we sympathize when she suffers pestilential heat and biblical thunderstorms, chiggers and hangovers, motel cockroaches so huge she sleeps in her car, food few Harvard graduates would dream of eating. ("A nightmarish chicken salad plate: a grisly mix of canned pears, bone and gristle swamped by mayonnaise . . . topped by a maraschino cherry.") Lost repeatedly, frustrated by maps and cloverleafs and traffic cops, betrayed by her tape recorder, this Ivy League intellectual turns out to be an endearing screwup. Sly storytellers mesmerized her with small talk and never delivered the goods. The great Ray Hicks on his mountain was as hard to track as the snow leopard, and he never—in spite of a hundred-dollar appearance fee—actually told her the Jack tale she came for.

The epic quest was something of a shipwreck. Petro might have cut her losses by turning her book into a comic adventure, a Hollywood road movie: The Perils of Pamela. If she had buried her psychohistory of the South in the red-clay landfill where it belongs, I wouldn't need to disparage her banal conclusion that race is the common wound beneath all Southern narrative. In the Appalachians, where the best stories are preserved, slaves were even scarcer than Confederate patriots. To a mountaineer, The War was a deadly nuisance and race was not life's central reality, as it must have been in Charleston, but a remote abstraction indeed.

The Southerner yields to no one when it comes to denial, a gift that shielded him and damaged him, too. But he's no innocent savage who lives an unexamined life on the thin ice of unexamined history, who unwraps his darkest secrets for any rank stranger with a tape recorder.

Never tell the South you understand it better than it understands itself. Like Brer Rabbit, it may outfox and outlast you. Our indigenous storytellers have a penchant for using found materials. One of them is already convulsing audiences with the story of plucky Pamela, chiggers and all, choking on her chicken salad.

The Southerner always tended to believe
with his blood rather than his intellect.

—Marshall Frady, *Southerners*

Son of a Preacher Man

MARSHALL FRADY (1940–2004)

I never met Marshall Frady, though we knew so many of the same
people it seems uncanny that I missed him. We even survived the
same apprenticeship as writers, among the hopeful anonymous at
Time-Life and Post-Newsweek. I can imagine what he went through
at those places. My own prose style, naturally expansive, still turns
timid at times from the savage abuse it suffered at the hands of news-
magazine editors, some of them—luck of the draw—not sagacious
old pros but tone-deaf philistines and phrase-butchers. Frady alone
betrayed no scars. He managed to nurse his polysyllabic style through
the lean years and see it bloom extravagantly under kinder editors,
most notably Willie Morris at *Harper's*.

It was a prose too exuberant to die. An ironic consequence of
Frady's untimely death last spring, at sixty-four, is that his books—
seven, including a recent Penguin biography of Martin Luther King
Jr.—began to receive more of the attention they always deserved.
Readers rediscovered a mode of English expression like no other,
North or South. Or rather, like one other. A steadfast son of the
South—a Baptist preacher's boy from Georgia—Frady never for-
swore his debt to William Faulkner, to Faulkner's native themes and

obsessions and also to his headlong, tempest-tossed, punctuation-defying prose. He even spoke in what his friends called "Faulknerian patois."

"Faulkner is an experience that a lot of Southern boys spend the rest of their lives trying to recover from," Frady wrote in his introduction to *Southerners*. He didn't try as hard as some. In New York they called his work New Journalism—because it was nothing like the old journalism, I suppose. Nobody bothered to compare it with *The Sound and the Fury*. I've seen word counts on some of Faulkner's sentences; I'm not young enough to take a week and count them on my own. But on page 282 of Frady's *Southerners*, in an essay titled "The South Domesticated," there's a 255-word sentence without one semicolon (and just three dashes). I won't even claim it's one of his longest.

Actually it's a damn fine sentence, too. You have to take care, when you write about Frady, not to write *like* Frady, or attempt it. As a stylist, he may have been one of the great subversive influences of his generation. Echoes of his hard-riding, whip-at-the-ready prose performances turned up in everything from free verse to postmodern fiction. But few novelists—and no one writing biography and literary journalism, as he did—ever equaled Frady's love for the sound of loaded clauses breaking like storm waves against the fragile sandbars of the reader's resistance.

There's every indication that he was born with that style, and employed stream-of-consciousness to write home to his parents from Bible camp. "He had it from the start, absolutely," recalls Joe Cumming, who hired Frady for *Newsweek*'s Atlanta bureau in 1966. "I asked him to write a quick bio sketch, you know, just so we'd have a writing sample in his file. He sat down and wrote seventeen pages that sounded like Shakespeare to me. It was a talent wasted at the bureau, of course—we knew he'd be moving on. But I used to defend his style against people who thought it was too exotic."

Apparently Frady aspired to live a life that matched his prose. At sixteen he ran off to Cuba to join the revolution—three times—and reached Havana once, but never managed to hook up with Fidel Castro or Che Guevara. "I never made it to the poetry going on in those mythic mountains," he wrote. Castro became a lifelong obsession. In 1973 Frady ran up a two-month, $17,000 expense account in Mexico City, pleading unsuccessfully with the Cuban embassy for a *Playboy* interview with Fidel. The two met at last in 1993. Frady was working on a biography of Castro when he died.

Marc Cooper of *The Nation*, who accompanied him on the Mexican expedition, describes the demonic disciplines of the picturesque writer in his prime: "He went to the pharmacy next door and bought a roll of amphetamine tablets. Then he bought a fifth of J&B and, at sunset, locked himself in his hotel room. The next morning I was stunned to see that he'd been up all night. The wrappers for the speed were empty. As was the bottle of scotch. Crumpled paper littered the room. 'Look, I've got it, I've got it,' he said, and handed me a single piece of paper."

"If anyone could be described as a hopeless romantic," says Joe Cumming, "it was Marshall."

Frady missed the revolution in Cuba but found one waiting for him back home. The Civil Rights Movement was the crucible for a generation of Southern journalists who remain among the bright lights of a rapidly dimming profession—to name a few would be to slight too many. Some of them took greater risks and delivered more battlefront dispatches, but no one articulated the experience more eloquently than Frady.

"By lucky accident," he wrote in *Southerners*, "I happened to be writing about the South at one of those climactic moments of truth when everything—past and present, inward and outward—suddenly glares into a resolution larger and more urgent than its ordinary aspect."

In an interview thirty years later, he evoked "the mighty moral drama of the movement in the '60s, which for a lot of journalists who covered it was like a kind of existential Damascus Road experience, a season of super-reality when good and evil somehow hit the bottom of the lungs in a way they never have quite since. . . ."

It's hard to ignore the suggestion that everything since Selma, since Memphis, had been anticlimax. I'm aware of the risks taken when you biographize the biographer, when you journalize the journalist. Marshall Frady anticipated his own psychobiographers. You can profile Frady just by quoting Frady; he never held much back. "Still secretly and irredeemably a kind of shabby romantic, still incorrigibly given to posturing," he says of himself at 30. "He had begun to be haunted that his epitaph might well be: 'His was a life of brave beginnings. . . .'"

I suspect Frady was angling for a better epitaph when he secured Jesse Jackson to preach his funeral. ("He could paint pictures with words," offered Jackson. "Even in his normal conversation he was a painter.") His long relationship with Jackson, who was famously fond of him and impatient with him, grew out of the Movement that provided them both with a season of epiphany and moral certainty, a "super-reality" after which many an encore seemed forced or false. Like Jackson, Frady was a gifted, ambitious individual who felt himself chosen for a higher calling that was not always recognized or encouraged. His biography of Jackson, *Jesse,* was a shrewd reassessment that went a long way toward rehabilitating a familiar figure who had been reduced—most unjustly, Frady argued—almost to a figure of fun.

Jesse balanced Jackson's outsized ego—"Not only does Jesse believe in God, Jesse believes God believes in him," one of Jackson's friends told Frady—against "a creative largeness of moral vision" and a "galvanic" capacity for personal connection he shared with only two public figures in Frady's experience: George Wallace and ("in his later days") Bobby Kennedy.

"Forever an unfinished hero," Frady called Jackson. But the most convincing depiction of heroism Frady ever wrote is his eyewitness account of Jesse's Gulf War mission to Baghdad in 1990—Jackson facing down Saddam Hussein and his secret police to extract hostages, life by life, with an unrehearsed display of compassion and resolve, cutting the kind of figure John Wayne could only fake for movie cameras. Hundreds were rescued. Iraqis were awed. But the State Department dismissed Jackson's feat with a curt "Thanks, pal," and the media, as usual, portrayed him as a showboating meddler.

That's the story of Jackson's life, as Frady told it: an ultimately tragic figure whose worst moments were magnified while his best were discounted. And Frady reminds us that all black leaders, even Reverend King, have had to clear a much higher bar to win respect. He loved Jackson, and identified with him, for the reach that exceeded his grasp—as the man who would be King, even Gandhi, in a country that wanted him to be Eddie Murphy.

But it was Jackson's personal magnetism that fascinated Frady, his rare ability to project and connect and make the faithful weep and shout. Ever since his father loomed above him with the holy scriptures on his tongue, the charisma of the "mass communicators, mass communers" had been Frady's special area of study. His major books comprise a gallery of charismatics. Only preachers and politicians, only those who risk everything on audience response need apply (and no Yankees). Jackson, Wallace, and Billy Graham had nothing in common except their unnatural grip on ordinary people—and their desperate need to exercise it.

As Frady saw him, Graham is a man of natural decency and sincerity, and very limited intelligence, whose simple faith and odor of sanctity were exploited by cynical presidents. Graham was "the indestructible American innocent," a country boy bewildered by his own celebrity. Frady compares him to Candide and to Melville's Billy Budd. Graham's great spiritual crisis was not a loss of faith in God but a loss of faith, after Watergate, in Richard Nixon. Another cleric described him to Frady as "God's own divine bumpkin."

George Wallace, "the greatest of the American demagogues, the classic of his species" was revealed to Frady as "curiously vague and weightless" in his private life, an empty suit, a political windup doll that only seemed alive when it was working crowds and pressing flesh. Like Graham, Wallace could never stand to be alone, and Frady found in him, as well, "a childlike naïvete." Frady called him "the stumpy, dingy, surly orphan of American politics," but he pitied Wallace, too, especially after the bullet in his spine ended the hands-on, "glandular" politicking that was all Wallace lived for.

Unlike most reporters, Frady wasn't probing for the flaws, for the feet of clay in his subjects' brogans; he took those for granted. What obsessed him was the populist mystery of their connection to crowds, and the high stakes they played for: power and high office, justice—souls.

Righteousness was his compass. Back through the Movement and the martyrdom of King, the dark feral passages of the race wars, back even to his infatuation with Castro and his stunned teenager's response to *For Whom the Bell Tolls,* Frady meant to stand on the side of the angels. In these "communicators" whose art transfixed him, he was always looking for a trace of the hero, for the divine spark. How much angel could he find, he always asked, in the ones the people followed?

This hunger for virtue is a Baptist, a Jesus thing, Frady tells us. And I thought, no, it's a small-town, middle-class thing—all of us brought up in quiet places by upright, thoughtful, honorable people start out on the side of the angels, wander offside and spend the rest of our lives trying to find it again. But I realized Frady's case was more acute when Billy Graham asked him, "What is your own spiritual standing?" I would have stammered and stared. But Frady answered promptly: "Well, I don't know that I have accepted Jesus exactly in the sense you would mean, but I believe in him, I love him, he's a living reality to me."

The last portrait in *Southerners* is of Will Campbell, the writer and outlaw Baptist minister Frady taxonomizes as "a fundamentalist gospel existentialist," and who was described to me as Frady's "father confessor." It happens that Reverend Campbell, who defies classification, is the man I might choose as my own confessor if I had enough holiness left in me to make regular pilgrimages to Mount Juliet, Tennessee. But I did make one recently.

"Frady is a hard man to describe," Campbell told me. "It was a different language he spoke, no matter what the subject. Who else used words like 'soliloquize' at breakfast? 'Let us retreat to the salt mines,' he'd say when he went to work. But there was an authentic person behind all those words; if he promised you something, you could put it in the bank.

"He was a big talker, a big liver, too, you know, but in a way he never left his father's fireside. He had that old Baptist commitment he was always affirming. Haunted by his faith. We won't meet another one like him."

Like all pure originals, Frady had his detractors. One prominent liberal journalist complained that "he was in love with the sound of his own words"—guilty as charged, I suspect—and that his supercharged syntax too often "lost it on the curves." The charges against him seem to boil down to a single judgment: whether the gorgeous language overwhelms the message or obscures the personalities.

If my vote counted, I'd say, "Not often." Whose book would you read, the writer who notes Congressman Mendel Rivers's "soft Southern drawl"—and couldn't in all likelihood tell a Charleston drawl from the Richmond version—or the one who describes "a mossy purr . . . an ambient and wraith-breathed delivery, as elusive and stealthy as fog rippling slowly over a swamp of hyacinths and water moccasins"? It's your call.

"The 'how' becomes the 'what' when you read Marshall," says his friend Franklin Ashley. "The way it's put together is inseparable from the story itself. No one else approached that fusion."

There's a prophetic element, too—not biblical but wry and Menckenesque. It was Frady, twenty-five years ago, who predicted that the adjective *Christian* would one day describe everything from theme parks to nightclubs to rock 'n' roll. His eyeball-to-eyeball with Saddam Hussein is worth reading, too. But Frady's gallery of saints and sinners, beginning with *Southerners*, is the visionary achievement like nothing else in the literature. To my ear, it's a Song of the South sung with near-perfect pitch, neither sweet nor sour, seasoned righteously with salt and soul.

If an individual from Wisconsin claims the Badger State had one just like Earl Long or Mendel Rivers—or George Wallace or Martin Luther King Jr.—my response is to say, "The hell it did, buddy," and refer him to the collected works of Marshall Frady. They should be required reading as long as the South makes a point of being the South—a point perhaps finite in time—and afterward for anyone who wants to know what it was like to live in "this peculiar dream-province of the Republic," as he called it, during the tumultuous half-century when Frady stood his never-wordless watch.

The Other Appetite

THE LITERATURE OF LUST

"There are two fundamental urges in nature: the desire to eat and the desire to reproduce one's kind. Which of these two impulses is the stronger depends somewhat on the individual and somewhat on the circumstances surrounding the individual—that is, it is apt to vary with the quality of the food and of the women. There are, Zaner shows, men who would rather eat than reproduce, and there are isolated cases of men who would rather reproduce than eat."

This voice of science is the inestimable E. B. White in Chapter 8 ("Frigidity in Men") of the recently reissued *Is Sex Necessary?* a best-selling parody of contemporary sex studies that White coauthored with James Thurber in 1929. The dry, cool, genteelly sexist tone White achieves here belies the fact that he was not yet thirty. Alternating chapters with the older, slightly more worldly and antic Thurber—who also contributed fifty of his indescribable minimalist drawings—White set a gold standard for writing about The Other Appetite that no subsequent American has eclipsed. My own prejudice is that sex is a great prose-destroyer—the more seriously you take it, the harder you try to immolate your inhibitions and pierce the pulsing core of human desire, the sooner you stumble into Silhouette Romance, coarse pornography and unintentional comedy.

Pedestrian prose often suffers from venereal diseases of its own device. For all but the most inspired stylist, sex acts are narrative animals that refuse to be housebroken. Banish them from the parlor, is my honest advice. Observe from a discreet distance and leave the rough bits out in the barnyard from whence they came. Try to name great books that were powerful *because* of their sexual content. Then quickly name fifty failures that were embarrassing, even disgusting because the sex scenes read as if too much blood has been diverted from a lecherous author's brain.

The foreword to the new HarperCollins edition of *Is Sex Necessary?* was written by John Updike, who loves the book but has not, in his own fiction, always profited from its circumspect example. Thurber and White will be taxed for unbearable lightness by heavy-breathing moderns, now that even "literary" memoirs relate grim sexual relations with animals, family members, and electrical appliances. In fact their book satirizes courtship and the war between the sexes, and scarcely sex, per se, at all. The prime example of "Frigidity in men" that White explores in Chapter 8 is "recessive knee"—a wary male's reluctance to maintain casual knee contact with the female, for fear that she may be pursuing an agenda. But for all its facetiousness, antiquated chastity and pre-feminist, pre–Queer Studies sensibility, the book betrays the confusions and insecurities of young men just entering the lists of love, in no less a Babylon than the New York City of the 1920s.

Beneath its mock pomposity and extended goofing (a young man seeking his sex education in the proverbial "gutter" will meet, in the gutters of Cincinnati, a man leading a tame stork with a live baby in its bill), timid truths are lurking—perhaps even in White's sly note on men who would rather eat than mate. In a rather alarming recent book titled *Sex in the South: Unbuckling the Bible Belt,* author Suzi Parker describes Columbia, South Carolina, as a hotbed of after-hours excess where a local specialty is sex mixers featuring BBWs—Big Beautiful Women, or what a paleo-chauvinist like Thurber might have called "whoppers." But the last time I prowled the streets of Columbia, it was in the entourage of Mississippi's intrepid Foodfather, John T. Edge, and what we were seeking was not the heart of Saturday night but the perfect pimento cheeseburger. If anyone sampled a Whopper that night, it must have been at Burger King.

Parker's is not a book that belongs on a shelf with White and Thurber. She confesses that she grew up on *Cosmopolitan* and Judith Krantz novels, and it shows. The gutters of Cincinnati offer a more useful sex education than Judith Krantz and Helen Gurley Brown. But give Parker credit for gripping the bull—the Minotaur, the mythic Southern libido—by its very horns. And for talking her way into Stygian sin cellars that you and I wouldn't enter without a pistol and a pit bull.

Expanding on the tradition of Erskine Caldwell, who convinced Yankees of another era that starving sharecroppers coupled like rabid weasels along the highways of Dixie, Parker diagnoses epidemics of satyriasis and nymphomania that consume our every class, race, and creed. I'm speechless when she calls the South "a surreal bubbling cocktail of unbridled desire," and "the nation's premier sexual hothouse . . . a place where an adulterous couple will knock it out as a prelude to church and then spend the sermon exchanging knowing looks across the pews." (Surely not Episcopalians?) Or when she celebrates my own Baptist, Bush-loving North Carolina as a mecca for swingers and wife-swappers: "From the top of the state near the Virginia border to the most Southern part that edges South Carolina," Parker writes (most infelicitously), "North Carolina is a hideaway for switching partners."

Surely she means contra dancing. Parker's South is not my South; her North Carolina is not my North Carolina. Which doesn't mean, of course, that hers do not exist. If a man ends up with a cheeseburger instead of a big girl's room key, it doesn't mean that he's less than a man in full. If some of us put less sex in what we write and prefer less in what we read, it doesn't always follow that our lusts are tepid ones, or that our stories are too tame to tell. Generalization fails dismally when the subject is sexuality—it is the classic case of the blind men and the elephant. One man's Vesuvius is the next man's lava lamp. A consistently true thing about sex in print is that it teaches us more about the writer than about the perpetual mystery of sex. The same is probably true of researchers and counselors, from Alfred Kinsey to Dr. Ruth.

Philosopher Simon Blackburn, author of *Lust*, the current volume in the Seven Deadly Sins series (Oxford University Press), rests his attempt to rehabilitate Lust, "the black sheep of the family" of sins, on our firm understanding of its infinite variety. Good sex, the perfect meeting of minds and loins he describes as "Hobbesian unity," is "variably realized"—"That is, as with a conversation, there is no one way of doing it. This is why sex manuals are so dreadful, except for unfortunates who do not have a clue anyway, and need the equivalent of '69 Ways to Have a Conversation.' . . . It is not the movements, but the thought behind them, that matter to lust."

Blackburn, the droll scholar, is a rare self-mocking sex authority who belongs in the distinguished company of Thurber and White. His puns are intentional: "Nobody would be asked to give a lecture on lust until of an age when time and experience have blunted its fierce prick." (As opposed to the jacket copy for Rosemary Daniell's steamy *Confessions of a (Female) Chauvinist*, which praises the author for exploring "the bedrock issues defining women in contemporary society.")

Lust, which I recommend, is even Southern by a modest stretch. Blackburn, an Englishman ("Other nationalities are amazed that we English reproduce at all"), taught at the University of North Carolina during the 1990s but has recently repatriated to take a chair at Cambridge. Here in the Swinger State, where sexuality is disputed between disciples of Jerry Falwell, Howard Stern, and Andrea Dworkin, Blackburn's urbane and tolerant voice will be sorely missed. His legacy to me is twofold. He rejects all pretense of neutral androgyny and speaks—come what may, like Thurber and White before him—as a heterosexual male. "For a long time now," he writes, "the discourse of sexuality has belonged to women and to other groups who feel they need to explain or justify themselves, notably gays." Best of all,

Blackburn acknowledges, with a touch of pride, the defining tradition of Eros in England: "We tend not to make a fuss."

Be not embarrassed by testosterone, nor by restraint. In one essay that attracted unfavorable comment, I confessed that Madonna—who is, or was, essentially a budget burlesque show—aroused me infinitely less than my cherished fantasy of "a Yeats scholar in a demure wool dress, whispering something mildly suggestive in my ear as we pass on the library steps." I added that nothing in Madonna's repertoire would inflame me like a chance to watch Claire Bloom water her delphiniums.

That's my contribution to erotic literature, one that dates me like a bronze plaque on a blackened statue of General Longstreet. I stand by it, and unless you can read between the lines, it's all you'll ever learn about my libido from me.

Is this Victorian? Does it reek of a certain class, or race? Is it Southern? I always believed that a gentleman took the public stance that he had no sex life, would perform poorly if one were offered to him, and expected no improvement unless some woman came to pity him in the extreme. (We were invited, I suppose, to assume the opposite about this sorry celibate, but any hint of boastfulness or aggression was white trash, K-Mart, and worse.) Naturally this modest gentleman required the same reticence from his women.

The irrepressible Suzi Parker has her own twist on this: "The deal in Dixie is that everybody does it but no one talks about it." Or writes about it, used to be. There's scant precedent for dealing with the rebel who *does* talk about it, like Suzi Parker. The twelfth word in Parker's book is "fuck" (and the thirteenth is "me"). Though every honest man loves a woman with a dirty mind—she's a rare jewel of her gender—a dirty mouth is something else.

Along with the myth of unblemished womanhood, the "pedestal-ism" White and Thurber lampooned in 1929, the much-violated code of sexual "Omerta" is losing its grip in the modern South—and its most flagrant violators have been women. The stark-nekkid erotic memoir is a genre now, almost a cliché. Parker's in the second or third generation of good old girls who will bare it all for a book contract, or a grudge. Authors like Florence King, Rosemary Daniell, and Vicki Covington perform at a much higher literary level than saucy Suzi, but they share her defiant spirit and her contempt for Southern "ladies" who starch their knickers.

Confessional memoir is billed as a natural backlash to centuries of sexual repression, not only the Bible Belt injunction against doing it at all but the maternal interdiction against doing it without a goal and a strategy. The Southern male takes a pounding in these books: Daniell undressed a semi-anonymous James Dickey in *Fatal Flowers*, when he was living, then stripped him again in *Confessions of a Female Chauvinist*, after he was dead. She even rated him a "3" on a sexual scale of 10. No one felt sorry for the poet, who once prescribed a leather strap and a jar of Vaseline for teaching women "the essence and particularities of love." Still, The best mating advice for any young person, male or female, is "Never sleep with a writer"— though of course I've been doing it for twenty-four years.

Sex will never be dignified, but it can and should be private. It's an embarrassing link to our simian ancestors but also one of our great improvements upon them. Though we share 99.4 percent of our DNA with chimpanzees, our exclusive .6 percent must be responsible for romantic love, idealized marriage, erotic nuance and the hominid novelties we call privacy and dignity. Reality TV, radio shock jocks, Internet pornographers, and hog-wild swingers intend to eradicate that small but critical evolutionary advantage as quickly as they can.

It's my tentative belief that these lethal viruses are of Yankee or West Coast origin, and not native to the South. Perhaps when the backlash against the patriarchy has run its course, Southern men and women of a certain perception will find common cause against a toxic culture that anathematizes modesty, subtlety, and discretion.

I've been looking for reasons to believe. In New York I took comfort from *And Tell Sad Stories of the Death of Queens*, a previously unproduced play by Tennessee Williams. Its heroine is an outrageous drag queen who beneath two layers of concealment—one of mascara, the other of male physiology—is just a sweet girl looking for love.

Violence occurs onstage, sex occurs off—not something you can count on, these days, in a New York theater.

Weren't serious Southern writers always, at some level, on the side of sentiment? Few offered their readers more sex per volume than the late and bitterly mourned Larry Brown. Euphemism was heresy to Larry. He believed in rendering violence and the entire spectrum of human ugliness exactly as it appeared to him, without cosmetic surgery. Sex acts recur in his fiction, as they tend to in life. Yet sex is the least graphic of his facts of life; on occasion his lovers even take a sentimental movie fadeout (*Fay*, p. 123: "'C'mere,' she said softly"—Curtain).

Even the most bizarre characters in *The Rabbit Factory*, like one-legged Miss Muffett and the murderer Domino—who's ultimately castrated and eaten by lions—are longing not for sexual friction and orgasm but for something finer, deeper ("There had to be more to it than what he and Doreen had done," Domino thinks, as the lion crushes his head. "That was just fucking. He'd had plenty of fucking. That was all animals had. Just making little animals."). They're longing, at last, for that Hobbesian unity—for tenderness.

Faulkner and the Mosquitoes

The ridicule of literary theorists is a poor diversion, roughly as challenging—and as appetizing—as shooting box turtles with a machine gun. These scarcely moving targets, stumbling under their heavy burdens of calcified jargon and unjustified self-regard, have been perforated, pulverized, atomized by a battalion of smirking assailants across the light-year-wide intellectual spectrum from Harold Bloom to Rush Limbaugh. Since no one outside the academy ever reads them, there's little incentive to blast them—their heads and pelts make trophies of no great prestige. Perhaps the last notable coup against their dismal tribe was counted in 1996 by NYU physicist Alan Sokal, who wrote a parody of cutting-edge theory in its own baroque patois, "privileging" and "valorizing" everything in firing range, and was rewarded with respectful publication in one of theory's own journals of record.

Sokal's jape, celebrated in the late lamented *Lingua Franca*, presaged the breakup of the Duke University English department, where many of the celebrities of theory's brief heyday had been cloistered in style. Duke's star-heavy department was the envy of most fast-lane humanities faculties until a devastating outside review (1998), by professors from even more elite schools like Stanford and

Chicago, targeted "low morale, ineffective leadership, a weak graduate curriculum and an inadequate intellectual mission." One of Duke's
theoretical heavyweights, Frank Lentricchia, also chose *Lingua Franca*
to chastise his own colleagues and his theory-besotted graduate students who refused to read primary texts. Within a few months, many
of Duke's big names had defected, and more traditional scholars had
reasserted their influence.

Duke's fleeting notoriety as the epicenter of postmodern heresy,
producing scholarly papers like "Jane Austen and the Masturbating
Girl," marked a kind of Golden Age for local satirists, for which we
were grateful. But by the spring of 2003, literary theory had fallen so
far from its primacy in the eighties and nineties that a public symposium on its future, held at the University of Chicago, failed to elicit
any obvious conviction that it had a future. A panel of prominent
critics including former Duke chairman Stanley Fish and his erst-
while prize recruit Henry Louis Gates, Jr. (along with paleo-Marxist
Fredric Jameson from Duke's French department, once crowned
"worst published writer in the world" in an Australian competition)
not only declined to defend their trademark theorizing but seemed
oddly reluctant to concede that they'd done it at all.

"I wish to deny the effectiveness of intellectual work," said the
slippery, ever-contrary Fish, whose most recent academic article argues that philosophy is irrelevant. (In his Durham days, Fish liked to
disparage my naïve reverence for free speech.) An amused observer,
reporter Emily Eakin of the *New York Times*, wrote a story full of condescension to these warriors of a vanishing Weltanschauung, portray-
ing them as much sillier than I know some of them to be. Evidently
the world of theory was ending with a whimper in the Windy City—
an end unimaginable a decade ago, when its enemies were publishing
Paul Revere–toned books like John Ellis's anguished *Literature Lost:
Social Agendas and the Corruption of the Humanities.*

"The era of big theory is over," Eakin decided. "The grand para-
digms that swept through humanities departments in the 20th century . . . have lost favor or been abandoned. Money is tight." But just
when you thought it was safe to read Kipling in the faculty lounge—

just when you thought it was safe to write a term paper without a nod to de Man or Derrida—a defiant theorist fires a broadside that leaves us wishing we'd buried "big theory" with a much bigger stake through its heart.

Franco Moretti, a professor of English and comparative literature at Stanford, has capped a career-long crusade for "text-free" scholarship with a manifesto titled *Graphs, Maps, Trees: Abstract Models for Literary History*. Writing in Britain's *New Left Review*, Moretti urges scholars to abandon reading altogether and get down to the serious task of counting books—counting and cataloging every book published, good, bad, or indifferent according to the outmoded culture of critical standards, since Gutenberg and the dawn of printing. Interpreted for the *Times* by the same astonished Emily Eakin, whose beat seems to be Quaint Campus Characters, Moretti envisions an English department of the twenty-second century with scholars who've never heard of Ahab or Ishmael, but who can tell you precisely how many seafaring novels were published between 1815 and the Civil War. Death of the author, death of the text, death of the English major —dawn of the database.

In his picture, wearing a huge red scarf draped at a rakish angle, Moretti looks more like a wry skeptic than a simpering idiot, so it's conceivable that he says these things just to attract attention and outrage easy marks like me and Harold Bloom, who of course declares Moretti "an absurdity." But if we take Professor Moretti at his word, we're obliged to wonder how many parents will pay $40,000 a year— or $40—to send junior to Stanford to count books. As ambitions go, Moretti's quantitative survey of world literature is a lot like teaching a bullfrog to play checkers. It would be a considerable and striking achievement, not easily dismissed. But what, to use theory's favorite word, does it signify?

Moretti's brainchild is another Caliban, the latest and least of the miscegenous monsters born when science tries to mate with the humanities. No doubt Harold Bloom is wise to sniff and roll his eyes and save his polemic for a more promising antagonist. But it's hard for a mere book-lover not to bare his teeth. Such a self-indulgent philistine could only flourish in our affluent, book-rich society, with so many literary choices that abundance breeds contempt. When all our books have been counted, what becomes of them then? Burned, pulped, shredded? Contrast this careless arrogance, this intellectual immaturity, with less "developed" societies where books are still holy, where reading is still a sacrament. Consider Azar Nafisi's *Reading Lolita in Tehran*, a story of young Iranian women who defied the ayatollahs, risking floggings and imprisonment for their secret reading group devoted to forbidden classics—Nabokov, Fitzgerald, Jane Austen, and Henry James. Consider a story from the weekly *Spekter* in Albania, a book-starved country where publishers shut down years ago and unemployed scholars sell precious classics to feed their children.

"I felt that I was committing the gravest crime," recalled one history teacher, fired without a pension, who had just sold *War and Peace* and *Anna Karenina* to a Tirana bookseller. He was caressing a favorite book, meticulously preserved in cellophane, as he confessed that his library of a thousand volumes had been reduced to a few dozen titles.

"There was no other solution," said Besnik R., now weeping. "But even if I am starving I will not give up my *Rubaiyat*."

Franco Moretti is also a teacher, a teacher who says wistfully, "My dream is of a literary class that would look more like a lab than a platonic academy." Read these two interviews and imagine that your community could only support one teacher. Which of these teachers would you feed—the one thriving in Palo Alto or the one starving and clutching his *Rubaiyat* in Tirana?

Pardon my sentimental subtext. We won't cleanse the academy of opportunists and philistines by sneering at all postmodern criticism, as if the last word on literature went to Lionel Trilling long ago. Some of the theory lumped under "deconstruction" is devilishly clever—the linguistics more than the politics—and by no means irrelevant. Unless you think The Canon was sent down from Mount Sinai, you concede many of the theorists' basic premises: that no author writes untainted by the biases of his time and place and class, that many "great" books (most notably the Bible) were weapons in great power struggles, that each reader brings unique history and unique interpretation to each text. In other words, each book and each reading is an imperfect, unpredictable act of communication. (And of course straight white males always controlled the printing presses, along with the learning that kept them rolling.)

The trouble with these revelations was that they were too transparent to support such a weight of ideology. They faded into a fistful of flaccid truisms long before the scholars who built careers on them were ready to retire. No doubt it's boredom, spawned by exhausted theory, that provokes weird post-postmodern rebels like Franco Moretti. It's a great misfortune for readers and students that so many misfits with their hearts in the sciences have been drawn, unaccountably, to the study of literature. This was the subject of a recent lecture at the University of North Carolina by Joyce scholar Weldon Thornton, who argued that "the confusion and loss of orientation in present-day Western culture have resulted from our deferring to ideas that are essential to scientific empiricism but are antithetical to human experience and values."

And toxically antithetical, Thornton stresses, to literary scholarship. The miracle, the mystery, the infuriating superiority of literature derives, always, from precisely what can't be predicted or analyzed or quantified. It's the common chord certain writers strike, a chord audible across all frontiers of time, class, culture, race, and gender, linking not only writer and reader but generations of writers and readers.

Isolating that chord—defining genius or inspiration or "greatness"—is and has always been like capturing moonbeams. But the only critics worth reading are the ones who try. It's tone-deaf critics, tin ears who can't hear it or share it, who despise genius and deny that it exists. Even talent offends them. The thwarted artists, the clever ones who can think but can't sing—these are the enemies of literature. Books are all power and oppression and propaganda, they insist, and the words of the immortals bounce off their thick armor like hail off a school bus.

Even children know a good line when they hear one. But I've listened to a scholar deconstruct Shakespeare line by line—court intrigue here, anti-Semitism there, all the remote gossip and partisan pettiness of Elizabethan London revealed to this learned man—but the towering, timeless language seemed invisible to him, like a man picking berries unaware of a grizzly bear looming over his shoulder.

You can never define great literature, you can only watch it work. Nothing can contain it, not even its native tongue. Translations may vary in quality, but language is an insubstantial barrier for a writer who can play the major chord. Take William Faulkner and the Hispanics. Halfway through Margaret Sayers Peden's wonderful translation of *Sepharad*, by the Spanish novelist Antonio Muñoz Molina, I came across a character who was reading *The Wild Palms*. I thought of Jorge Luis Borges, who honored Faulkner, his contemporary, above all North American writers.

"Faulkner has been compared to Dostoevsky," Borges wrote in a 1938 review of *The Unvanquished*. "This is not unjust. But the world of Faulkner is so physical, so carnal, that next to Col. Bayard Sartoris or Temple Drake the explicative murderer Raskolnikov is as slight as a prince in Racine. . . . There are books that touch us physically, like the closeness of the sea or of the morning. This—for me—is one of them."

And in the footnotes to Borges's *Selected Non-Fictions*, I discovered that Borges translated *The Wild Palms* into Spanish—most likely the same translation the Muñoz Molina character would have been reading in Andalusia decades later. Borges's translation, the footnote added, "was enormously influential on young Latin American novelists such as Gabriel Garcia Marquez."

Here rambling coincidence flowered into the kind of reader's epiphany Franco Moretti might never understand. The other book I've been reading is the memoir by García Márquez, *Living to Tell the Tale*. It begins with a wretched journey the writer takes with his mother in 1950, across the vast swamp Colombians call Cienega Grande: "The bloodthirsty mosquitoes, the dense heat, the nauseating reek of the channel mud churned up by the launch as it passed, the frantic back-and-forth of sleepless passengers who could find no place to sit in the crush of people—it all seemed intended to unhinge the most even-tempered nature."

García Márquez endures this terrible night chain-smoking cheap cigarettes made of black tobacco—and reading *Light in August*. He describes the book's grip on him as "the quicksands of Yoknapatawpha County," and William Faulkner as "the most faithful of my tutelary demons."

The pestilential swamps, the mud and mosquitoes, the twenty-three-year-old writer drunk on Faulkner in a world infinitely remote from the "postage-stamp of native soil" that inspired *Light in August*, the knowledge that this pretentious chain-smoking boy, as he describes himself, will one day write his own great novels of a godfor-saken place and win his own Nobel—this is the DNA of literature. If the books themselves aren't enough, if like Professor Moretti you need a project, try to discover just who was reading whom on which occasion. Begin in Mississippi and rewind the thread that in this case links two great languages, four nations on three continents, two No-bel Prize winners (and who cheated Borges of his prize?), and three generations of remarkable writers. You may begin to comprehend this fabulous beast that eludes most theorists: literature as a living, warm-blooded thing, a nigh-immortal organism that embodies all the his-tory and hopes of the cultures where it evolves. A thing big enough, generous enough to embrace the lot of us, writers and readers—the veiled women in Tehran and the hungry teacher in Tirana, the laure-ate-to-be sweating nicotine in the North Colombian swamps.

On this great body of living literature, theorists are an ephem-eral nuisance, an irritant like the mosquitoes. (Faulkner knew mos-quitoes; Faulkner wrote *Mosquitoes*.) Years ago in the Okefenokee Swamp, paddling a canoe through swarms of huge bloodsucking in-sects, I learned the value of stoic forbearance. If you're tough enough not to scratch your bites, you find no trace of them in the morning.

The Song

Gather at the River

THE O BROTHERHOOD

In Grundy, Virginia, where Ralph and Carter Stanley once played blue-grass on the roof of the concession stand at my wife's uncle's drive-in theater, Joel and Ethan Coen's *O Brother Where Art Thou?* has been drawing customers rarely seen in the village, far less at the movies. They pack in their own popcorn and sandwiches; refreshment prices, even in Grundy, are by sane country standards outrageous.

It's not clear that these are direct descendants of the people in John Sayles's film *Matewan*—set in the same coalfields—who show up with their squirrel rifles to thwart the coal company goons. "Are those the mountain people?" asks one awed witness, and another replies, "Those are the *hill* people—even the hill people are afraid of the mountain people."

But a Grundy High English teacher didn't recognize many of them from class.

"I don't guess they're familiar with Homer or James Joyce" she said *(O Brother,* like Joyce's *Ulysses,* is based loosely on *The Odyssey),* "or Mississippi cotton fields either. But they applaud every song, and when they hear the Stanley Brothers break into 'Angel Band,' well . . ."

In music stores all over the country, fans without squirrel rifles have been demanding CDs by the Soggy Bottom Boys, a trio that exists only on a motion picture soundtrack. That soundtrack, recorded for the Coens' film by T Bone Burnett, is the first CD ever to top Billboard's country album charts with absolutely no help from the music industry, which is so hardwired into selling premasticated "young country" pop-pap that its robot radio conceded no air time to *O Brother* even when the album hit Number One.

In today's Soviet-style music market, charts and sales are never supposed to vary from a master plan concocted by a dozen gold-chained aural pornographers in Nashville, New York, and LA. This corporate Kremlin has redefined country music as tarted-up fluff, as Faith Hill singing "Breathe" against a Vegas-style light show with a wind machine blowing her hair—a ghastly moment on national TV when I literally cringed and imagined Minnie Pearl mocking it all on the Grand Ole Opry, with the wind blowing her hat across the stage.

"'Contemporary' country is a gooey, soulless mix of skinny women in slutty outfits, pinheaded guys in big hats, headset microphones and videotape," rages critic Walter Howerton, Jr., of Kentucky. "It's music to look at—no-risk suburban music coming from no place in particular."

After a month at Number One, *O Brother* was still missing from the airwaves, dismissed by CMT types as a freak hit, the one-in-a-million chart-crasher spawned by a major motion picture. Committed to selling canned sex, canned attitude, and canned aggression to sulky children and hormone-ravaged adolescents, the commissars reject even the possibility that adults might respond in commercial numbers to well-made, deep-rooted, deeply felt native music.

Is *O Brother*'s shocking breakthrough—it quickly went platinum—liberating evidence that the commissars are wrong, that authenticity will sell itself? "Authentic," abused by lazy critics of everything from rap groups to deck furniture, is a dignified adjective that may have lost its pedigree. Probably authenticity isn't something we can ever measure or quantify. What is it that Vermeer epitomizes and Andy Warhol disparages? Any fool knows George Jones is authentic and Garth Brooks less so, but who could have a coherent argument about it?

Something like a miracle has occurred, nonetheless. Someone played a true, pure note that hadn't been heard in the marketplace in a long, long time. And here and there among the cattle, among the captive consumers herded ruthlessly from fraud to fraud, from buzz to buzz by the corporate culture cowboys, tired heads looked up and listened, and something almost spiritual, almost human appeared in their ungulate eyes.

After you've heard Allison Krauss and Ralph Stanley, can you ever go back to Faith Hill and Tim McGraw? Is the power of country's finest musicians and its strongest, truest music any match, in the long run, for the power of the jerks who own the jukebox? Enjoy the battle won, hedge your bets on the war, and never underestimate the staying power of trash culture and bad taste.

As a motion picture, O Brother is equal parts endearing and aggravating. Expect ruffled feathers in Dixie when a Christian baptism corresponds to Homer's island of the Lotus Eaters and a robed Klansman "sings" Ralph Stanley's sublime "O Death." As usual the Coen brothers are twisting someone's tale. Only the Coens can tell us whether they're tormenting dumb Yankees who think O Brother's caricatures represent documentary footage of the modern South, or Southerners horrified to see their most embarrassing ancestors on parade as comic stereotypes—or both.

"Hollywood says Southerners are retarded," said musicologist Bill Malone, "but we sure can sing."

What O Brother gave us to look at we can fight about forever; what it gave us to listen to we can only receive like a sacrament. You may not appreciate the film unless you understand that it's a musical, a folk opera. The music came first, as Burnett and the Coens have explained repeatedly, and scenes and characters were keyed to the songs. Unless the music grips you, the movie makes no sense. If you're optimistic that the culture gulf between Mississippi and Manhattan will be bridged in the next hundred years, don't read Anthony Lane's dismissive review of O Brother in The New Yorker. Lane barely mentions the music, a gaffe as stupefying as reviewing Moby-Dick without mentioning the whale.

As every culture critic decries the death of legitimate communities, T Bone Burnett's real miracle, as I've come to think of it, is that his soundtrack defines a genuine community and expands it to millions who didn't know they belonged until they heard this recording. If this musical family excludes New York's smug tastemakers, it's big enough to embrace both Grundy mountaineers, who kept the faith all along, and fugitive media slaves who discover lost roots when they hear the Soggy Bottom Boys. In principle the O Brotherhood includes most African Americans, most of the South, the whole length of the Appalachians, and a wide swath of rural America. And the congregation includes a passionate chorus of writers and scholars, those Southerners most immune to popular culture and group enthusiasms.

"I think 'You Are My Sunshine' was the first song I ever heard," says Virginia poet R. H. W. Dillard. "If this is your culture, this music has the grip of myth, of racial memory. You listen and you know who you are."

One night I was listening to Antonin Kubalek playing Czech piano music—Smetana, Janacek—and loving it (Crowthers are nothing if not catholic in our musical tastes—my father used to alternate Erroll Garner and Jerry Lee Lewis). But the *O Brother* disk replaced Kubalek, and by the time the Cox Family started singing "I Am Weary," I felt as if I'd had a blood transfusion—I was purged of all things toxic, foreign, or superfluous and restored to some primordial state of grace.

It must have been my first rush, in a long, logic-hobbled life, of something that felt like chauvinism. I was proud to be a member of whatever group this music defines. A middle-class hillbilly raised by Unitarians, kin to no Southern Baptists or born-agains that I know of, I considered for the first time that maybe *I* could hear "the voice of the Lord God walking in the garden in the cool of the day." (Memory: "Man of Constant Sorrow"—a folky version by Peter, Paul and Mary—was my undergraduate theme song, a dirge I droned so relentlessly that my college roommate nicknamed me "MOCS.")

Those of us thus blessed warn ourselves not to overproselytize. I was recommending the soundtrack to an old friend, an urban Yankee and a Jew. Then I thought, my god, all that gospel. Will he think I've been down to the river at last, a doddering old pilgrim fresh washed in the Blood of the Lamb? But then I thought—hey, the Coen brothers aren't Presbyterians. Some say you won't rise up shouting unless this music's in your bloodstream, recorded somewhere on your life tape. But maybe the ancient rich brew of guts, grief, and gospel intoxicates almost anyone who actually buys recorded music for the way it sounds and not for the hype it rolls in on.

My wife and I agree: *O Brother*'s the first CD we ever owned that didn't wear out its welcome after fifty plays, that actually seems to improve. At the Merle Watson bluegrass festival, Dolly Parton offered a trademark endorsement: "I think it's great for the old music and for all of us who love to play it—just so they don't start calling me the Soggy Bottom Girl."

But we all yield to the testimony of Susan Ketchin, Georgia-born scholar/musician, author of *The Christ-Haunted Landscape,* singer with the Angelettes and the Tarwater Band:

> This music is haunting and haunted. It reaches in and grabs your heart, scrapes your bones. It makes me tremble. Like the girl in the Appalachian legend who fiddled on the mountainside until she died, like the culture she came from, this music is touched by madness. Yet the emotional wells it draws upon are deeper than any cultural differences. They're hidden caverns, underground rivers of sorrow. I've been to see *O Brother, Where Art Thou?* five times now and counting. The first time I experienced these old songs, these voices, I wept. I want this to be the soundtrack for my funeral.

Amen, sister. If we could add jazz, *O Brother* would pay elegant homage to every original strain of music this country has produced. "Epic songs," T Bone Burnett calls them, and what he's put together by a stroke of intuitive genius is not a sampler, not a mere anthology of vintage Southern music, but a genuine piece of the rock: the bedrock, the Rock of Ages where we secretly long to cling.

Movies, Mules, and Music

"What makes the South southern?" is a question that still provokes serious debate among Southerners. At one literary symposium, English professor Jerry Leath Mills of the University of North Carolina dismissed a cartload of leaden theory with the results of his own extensive research: "There is indeed a single, simple, litmus-like test for the quality of Southernness in literature. . . . The test is: Is there a dead mule in it?"

Mills followed his nose from text to text and found the Southern literary landscape so littered with the carcasses of these poor brutes that scholars of a future century might mistake the mule for a sacrificial animal, like the bulls and rams of yore. A scholarly performance more accurately styled "decomposition" than "deconstruction," Mills's essay "Equine Gothic: The Dead Mule as Generic Signifier in Southern Literature of the Twentieth Century" exposes the fiction of William Faulkner as a serial boneyard for expired mules and turns up no fewer than fifty-nine mule fatalities in one novel, *Blood Meridian* by Cormac McCarthy. From the works of several dozen Southern authors Mills exhumed two hundred dead mules.

In Chapel Hill Professor Mills's theory inspired such enthusiasm that a saloon was named after it—the Dead Mule Club, where a friend of mine tends bar. But the Mule School of literary criticism stops short of arguing that Southern writers were fully conscious of this pungent recurring motif. Symbols and signifiers belong to the critics. For William Faulkner, living in Mississippi in an era when the mule population peaked at 350,000, a dead mule was just a sore place in a boy's memory, or a serious logistical challenge for men with ropes and shovels.

Film is a different animal entirely. Its demands are immediate, its signifiers charged with purpose. Compared with literature, which acquires generic trademarks and regional dialects through patient decades of cross-pollination, serious motion pictures communicate in urgent shorthand. Each successful filmmaker establishes his own vocabulary of images, linked on some Jungian level to a rich matrix of intelligible images—film's mother tongue. In a great modern film like Terrence Malick's *Days of Heaven,* images so overwhelm the dialogue that speech becomes superfluous.

"Words empower, images overpower," a film professor told us once, his way of saying a picture was worth a thousand words. When I tried my hand at screenwriting, I learned what Faulkner, Fitzgerald, and their peers all learned in Hollywood, to their chagrin: that onscreen a single startling image, brainchild of a semiliterate (if not idiot) savant of a director or cinematographer, invariably trumps twenty pages of meticulously crafted dialogue.

Jean-Luc Godard writes of Alfred Hitchcock:

People forget why Joan Fontaine was leaning over the cliff . . . and what Joel McCrea was up to in Holland . . . and why Janet Leigh stops at the Bates Motel. But they remember a car in the desert. They remember a glass of milk, the vanes of a windmill, a hairbrush. They remember a wine rack, a pair of glasses, a fragment of music, a set of keys. . . . Because through them and with them, Alfred Hitchcock succeeded where Alexander the Great, Julius Caesar, Napoleon and Hitler failed: in taking control of the universe . . . he was the greatest creator of forms of the twentieth century and it is forms which tell us, finally, what there is at the bottom of things; and what is art except that by which forms become style.

Film is such a potent medium that its greatest artists were often astonished by the power of their own creations. "You could look at it forever," Hitchcock said of one of his own compositions. Hitchcock created forms so eloquent they could bridge the gap between a warped genius and a mainstream audience; his screen world of polished surfaces, neurotic tension, concealed meaning and latent menace seemed vaguely familiar to most of us, if only from our dreams.

Where in film do we find a dialect of images that belong to the South alone? Though the "Southern" movie as a genre never developed the complex iconography that Hitchcock brought to the murder mystery or John Ford to the western, it was a native Southerner, D. W. Griffith of La Grange, Kentucky, who virtually invented the art of moving pictures. "He gave us the grammar of filmmaking," said Lillian Gish. The close-up, the pan, crosscutting, the flashback, the fade-in and fade-out were all Griffith innovations, and all were on gorgeous display in 1915, in his epic *Birth of a Nation*.

Unhappily Griffith, grandson of a Confederate general, was too much the Southerner—of his day—to leave a legacy we could build on. Master of the long shot but not the long view, Griffith, in *Birth of a Nation*, glamorized the Knights of the Ku Klux Klan and offered the white supremacist view of black Southerners as lazy, dumb, and dangerous. (To understand Hollywood films set in the South, at least since the sixties, just reverse Griffith so that most African Americans are brave and noble, most whites LD&D.)

As an influence on future filmmakers, *Birth of a Nation* was a technical goldmine and a psychological dead end. The South feels its shadow mainly as a source of caustic stereotypes, like the hooded chorus of singing, marching Klansmen in the Coen brothers' *O Brother Where Art Thou?* If I had to choose one early motion picture as a kind of Southern Ur-film, faithful to the spirit of a Southern experience and packed with images that enrich our screen vocabulary, I'd choose one that might surprise you.

There isn't a white face in it, no matter how hard you look. *Hallelujah*, released in 1929, was King Vidor's first talking picture. An all-black musical keyed to gospel songs and biblical allegory, cast with

Zeke is a Prodigal Son who can't control himself, whether he's chasing the holy spirit or a honky-tonk hussy from hell, a Magdalen/Delilah figure played deliciously by Nina C. McKinney, who had never before faced a camera. Zeke's world is split dramatically between sacred and profane, blues and gospel, Saturday night and Sunday morning. Here we begin to separate archetypes from stereotypes. Dixie's religious excesses were never a black monopoly. And a tragic lack of restraint shapes everything Southern, from Secession itself to Pickett's suicidal charge on Cemetery Ridge.

The most recent films set in the South, like *O Brother* and Maggie Greenwald's *Songcatcher,* just reinforce what we learned about Southerners from *Hallelujah:* that they're impulsive, superstitious, sentimental, none too cerebral, sometimes violent, but best of all musical, buried alive in the blues. The Coen brothers impose their corrosive satire on Depression Mississippi, Maggie Greenwald imposes well-intentioned but fumbling PC politics on the old-time Appalachians (signifiers: mules, moonshine, martin gourds). But both films go South primarily, and successfully, to celebrate our magnificent music.

No one claims folkloric authenticity for Vidor's film, not even for the score, which includes Zeke's Bing Crosby–style rendition of Irving Berlin's "At the End of the Road." But the rudiments of a Southern mythology are already there, along with a vocabulary of images—river baptism, revivals, singing convicts, paddle wheelers, canebrakes, cypress swamps, mule wagons, and boxcars—that nearly every filmmaker who passes this way will faithfully revisit.

Films will be a critical part of the historical record when a distinct South has vanished like its mules. What will history remember? Maybe that Southerners, black and white, could take credit for every major American contribution to the history of music, from jazz, blues, and gospel to country and western, bluegrass, mountain string bands, even rock 'n' roll. First among all the images that define the Homeland, as King Vidor seems to have known, are the fingers on the strings and the mouth strained wide open to let out the song inside.

actors of little or no experience, filmed in a "realistic" South of cotton gins, sawmills, and chain gangs, *Hallelujah* was a radical departure from any of Vidor's previous (or subsequent) films. At that time no established Hollywood director had ever packed his camera quite so far afield.

In fact, Vidor's choice wasn't as unfathomable as it seems at first glance. *Ol' Man Adam an' His Chillun,* a book of bible stories in Negro dialect published by Roark Bradford in 1928, was the inspiration for Marc Connelly's Pulitzer Prize–winning play, *The Green Pastures,* which opened in New York in 1930.

Chronology suggests that Bradford may have inspired Vidor as well. Black "folk" material was enjoying a modest vogue at the close of the Roaring Twenties. But *Hallelujah* preceded *The Green Pastures,* and as a native of Galveston, Texas, King Vidor was considerably more familiar with the "folk" in question. Vidor knew cotton fields, certainly, and the people—and mules—who worked them. *Hallelujah* begins and ends with a sentimental image of "them old cotton fields back home." In between, Vidor unloads a mule train of stereotypes from every white writer who ever tried to imagine the lives of black people. Chitlin-lovin',' flat-dancin',' honky-tonkin',' knife-fightin',' holy-rollin' natural folk, with their sainted mammies and popeyed picka-ninnies, here they are. Yet the picture begins to exert its charm once you realize that it was made with appalling ignorance but almost no condescension.

It's hard to believe that *Hallelujah* was promoted and generally accepted as an accurate representation of black life in the pre-Depression South. But to give Vidor half a chance, muzzle your contemporary political consciousness and remember that his Oscar nomination for this film came in 1930, a year when Southerners were credited with twenty-one lynchings. Vidor endowed his characters with dignity and tragic stature; he appealed these sinners' cases to a higher court. By ignoring the white devil, *Hallelujah* can focus on the real Devil incarnate, that devil inside Everyman. Vidor's protagonist Zeke (Daniel L. Haynes)—sinner, singer, evangelist, killer, convict, penitent—isn't struggling for his civil rights but for his soul.

Nashville

DOLLY AND THE SUBTERFUGITIVES

In his 1975 film *Nashville*—never praised and seldom mentioned in Nashville, Tennessee—Robert Altman scouted the borderlands between reality and fantasy in a city that's become less a state capital than a state of mind. Among American dream markets only Hollywood and Las Vegas bear comparison to Music City. And they don't, finally. Vegas will never be more than a pathogenic theme park in the desert; Hollywood, today, is little more than a brand name and an adjective that describes an inferior grade of motion picture.

Nashville is a real place as well as a showplace, a city where multitudes of people live unconnected to the country music industry and regard the herds of goggling tourists and would-be entertainers as a necessary evil. Vanderbilt University and Belle Meade—my aesthetic first choice, in its dogwood spring, of all America's wealthy neighborhoods—are aristocratic enclaves that long preceded the flood of music money and endure, resentfully, the compromises it imposes.

But Altman's nose did not deceive him when he chose Nashville as the locus for his disturbing psychoportrait of the American condition. This is a schizoid town where straight and twisted cohabit, where cultural opposites attract and repel. Tax attorneys write country songs on their palm pilots, everyone but the governor is in a band; Opry backup singers pursue M.F.A.s at Vanderbilt, the Harvard of the literary South. Poet Donald Davidson, the most unbending conservative of Vanderbilt's original Fugitives, wrote a country music novel, *The Big Ballad Jamboree*. A divided consciousness is standard equipment. Nashville presents a slippery surface, a backlit stage where the well-meaning and the predatory sing a strange duet.

I can't imagine what Vanderbilt expected when it invited fifty Southern writers for an April weekend billed as "A Millennial Gathering of the Writers of the New South." Press releases suggested that a new consensus might be forged, perhaps even an enduring brother/sisterhood to nurture Southern letters through the current Dark Age of American illiteracy.

But asking writers to work toward common goals is as realistic as hitching up a team of panthers to pull a hay wagon. It's not their fault. In fact I'd argue that there's an inverse relationship between the ability to create imaginative literature and the ability to participate in consensus. Every writer truly worth reading arrives with one essential: a skewed, eccentric, arresting way of looking at the world—an oblique angle of vision that defies assimilation.

Writers were never intended to network. At the first panel discussion, poet Dave Smith predicted the rocky road ahead: "We're people who live in the subjective, the specific, the singular," he objected. "We tend to recoil from generalizations."

In the general flight from generalization, writers harnessed to panels on race, class, and religion tended chiefly to testify. Unhappily, the religious and racial histories of fifty writers don't cut to the heart of the Southern experience any more cleanly than the histories of fifty bus drivers. Vanderbilt's Tony Earley, saddled with the hopeless task of summing up, dubbed his Nashville fifty (forty-four by my head count) the "Subterfugitives" and the "Conflagrarians." Southern writers may choke on abstractions, but self-mockery is an idiom where they excel.

Creative writers are never more useless than when you ask them to diagnose and prescribe, or to agree. But it was the Vanderbilt legacy, the Fugitive/Agrarian legacy, that must have dictated the form and themes of this gathering. It's a legacy that includes a quixotic faith in the power of poets. When *I'll Take My Stand* was published seventy years ago, most people whose opinion mattered were readers; when John Crowe Ransom, Robert Penn Warren, Allen Tate, and their friends embraced the role of social pathologists, they expected the wide world to sit up and listen. "It was necessary," Donald Davidson recalled at the Fugitives' reunion in 1956, "for the poets to make an attack upon society."

Such is the passage of time. If the poets attacked society now, every last one of them, in high dudgeon and close formation, how many years would pass before society would notice?

The weekend's most inspired program was a forum for "emerging writers," which offered a score of younger poets and novelists the chance to read their work. The praise they received from their elders was well deserved. My grim millennial prediction is that there will soon be far more first-rate writers, in the South and elsewhere, than first-rate readers to enjoy them.

An extreme bonding experience occurred in Nashville for writers accustomed to solitude. Death made a terrifying appearance at a media reception—a photographer collapsed and died among the white-wine drinkers, leaving literary and all other concerns looking wan and trivial, as Death will do. It fixed the weekend in our memories as nothing else could have, and reminded more than one witness of Altman's movie, in which all appearances deceive and nothing anywhere is actually under control.

Songs capture it better, that unstable reality where only the moment is knowable. You remember that Robert Altman let his actors write their own songs, theme songs to define their characters. Great country songs are often novels in miniature—Townes Van Zandt's "Pancho and Lefty," Robert Earl Keen's "The Road Goes On Forever," Matraca Berg's "Back When We Were Beautiful"—but Charles Portis was probably the last Southern novelist to capture the lyric immediacy of the best Nashville music.

A few songwriters shared the millennial bill at Vanderbilt, including Marshall Chapman, the towering cult goddess of redneck rock, who read from her Nashville memoir in progress. Bob McDill and Steve Earle, gold-standard songwriters of two different Nashville generations, sat on a panel with poets and marveled with the rest of us when a white poet testified that she was part African American, at least in the marrow of her bones, because her ancestors had black wet nurses.

Cross-fertilization between the world of books and the world of banjos isn't something you can take for granted. I was fortunate to have another engagement in Nashville, an invitation to lunch with Dolly Parton. Of the several writers in my family, one of them is Parton's favorite writer, and it's not me. After only thirty seconds in a crushing hammerlock, with my knee wedged firmly against her spine, my wife was kind enough to suggest that I join her and Dolly for lunch.

"I tried to dress down a little because you're a famous writer and I didn't want to look too cheap," says Dolly, who's wearing a black skirt slit almost to the hip and a purple sequined body sweater you could substitute for your Christmas tree. In the restaurant at Belle Meade Mansion, Dolly draws a round of applause from the lunch crowd and I turn and wave, a lame joke I've managed to keep in mothballs since 1969, when I walked into a Times Square restaurant in the entourage of Muhammad Ali. Two hard-breathing autograph vultures hit her before we reach our table, and Dolly treats them like kin, like royalty. The waitress requests a laying on of hands, and Dolly indulges her, too.

"They love for me to touch them," she tells us, without condescension. At fifty-four this is a woman who seems to love her work, her fans, and the considerable responsibility of being Dolly Parton. Her fans are polite but hungry to make a connection, any connection, and the lady isn't stingy with herself. She doesn't know that there isn't a "famous writer" on earth who gets spontaneous ovations at lunch.

Over at Vanderbilt, the New South writers were quick to agree that the marketplace starves talent and smothers genius. Every effort to rise above poverty seems to involve humiliating compromise with a ruthless establishment of philistines and mercenaries. But Dolly Parton is a walking, glittering rebuttal to all this grousing—in which I often join—that the cream never rises to the top.

Sometimes it rises. Parton came to Nashville as a starstruck teenager, went through the wringer like all the country girls, and found herself in the deep and troubled waters of celebrity. Instead of drowning, she learned to swim real well, thank you. Pressed into a Grand Ole Opry stereotype, a singing version of Lil' Abner's Daisy Mae, she took it to a level beyond imitation: "The dumb blonde act didn't bother me because I know I'm not dumb," she said, "—and I know I'm not blonde either."

As Dolly tells it, she was never shy about learning the business side of Music City, which has burned so many big talents to smoking ruins. "Many an old boy has found out too late that I look like a woman but think like a man," she recalls with a satisfied cackle.

Parton's latest CDs, returning to her roots in bluegrass, gospel, and old-time mountain string bands, have won extravagant praise from the most exacting critics; she also markets wigs and cosmetics, and Dollywood is ever-expanding. A serious reader and a philanthropist for literacy programs, Parton may be more comfortable with Nashville's splintered consciousness—pickers and poets, rural roots and rhinestones, high standards and hard cash—than anyone I've ever met.

She looks good and works at it. Parton approaches the word "real" with humor and artistic license. What you see is not exactly what time and gravity would have produced, unchecked. In her autobiography she gives her plastic surgeon's phone number and writes, "My spirit is too beautiful to live in some dilapidated old body if it doesn't have to.

"I look in the mirror, and if I see anything that doesn't look like Dolly, I tell 'em, 'Cut it off.'"

She doesn't know how long it takes to do her hair, she likes to say, because she's never there when it happens. Dolly wears her image the way Minnie Pearl wore her hat, like a favorite joke among old friends.

"Authentic" is a word you hear a lot around Nashville, from critics and publicists alike. I couldn't help noticing some new criteria for authenticity among Vanderbilt's "Writers of the New South." Where the Fugitive generation might have claimed ancestors who carried swords and planted cotton, these Subterfugitives claim recent ancestors who dipped snuff and lived without benefit of plumbing. One of my litmus tests for Southern authenticity would be the ability to appreciate the paradox of Dolly Parton: beneath a blinding surface of deliberate, exaggerated, self-satirizing artifice lurks one of the most engagingly authentic individuals in the Nashville pantheon.

When she restored her parents' old home place in the Smoky Mountains, Dolly designed her new toilets as a faux outhouse—a private joke and a wide-gauge irony she appreciates on the same level that Robert Penn Warren would have appreciated it. She just gets a much bigger kick out of doing it.

The Last Song of Father Banjo

Tommy Thompson was from West Virginia and he bore a certain resemblance to a mountain, or at least to someone who'd just come down from the mountain after talking to The Boss. He wore the weather on his shoulders.

"Tommy could close down the light and bring on the night," said his second wife, CeCe Conway, recalling the storms that rolled down the mountain. But when his sun was shining, birds broke into song and branches into blossom. After his final performance, well into his fatal illness, he called Conway and told her, "I have a sunny disposition—even still I guess."

She doesn't deny it. Tommy Thompson, the huge man his friends called Father Banjo and the Cajuns dubbed "Uncle Wide Load," died last winter at sixty-five, after nearly a decade of silent decline with an Alzheimer's-related dementia. Though he'd been off the stage for so long and virtually beyond communication for several years, the response to his death defined the critical difference between the weightless thing called celebrity and the rare personality that actually alters other people's lives.

"He was a wonder in many different ways," said his longtime piano player, writer Bland Simpson. "People would seek Tommy out—older, younger, men, women—to tell him, 'I play music because of you.' He imparted the love of music and inspired people. That's magic."

United by a fear that he might have died forgotten or underrated, friends, scholars, and musicians fell over each other trying to explain Tommy Thompson. It would have delighted and amused him. Tommy was not so much a humble man as a compulsively reflective one, a philosopher by training and inclination—possibly the only entertainer who ever claimed the seminal influence of both Ludwig Wittgenstein and Uncle Dave Macon. He took the long view.

"He was the philosophical graduate student always surrounding himself with unanswerable questions," recalled mandolinist Bertram Levy. "But when he got the banjo, it set him free."

In a cover story for the *Old-Time Herald*, written six months before Thompson's death, David Potorti collected a treasury of reminiscences by Tommy's musical collaborators. It's important to note that the Red Clay Ramblers, the band Thompson fathered and anchored for twenty-two years, must have the highest aggregate IQ and the most university degrees of any string band that ever lived. We might all covet eulogists like these. The quote that sticks with me is from Mike Craver, the Ramblers' original piano man.

"I remember watching him and thinking, if I had to describe a Shakespearean character, it would be Tommy. He was big then, and he had that kind of Falstaff quality to him—red hair, and a red beard. He was amazing looking, and the word that comes to mind is probably charismatic. You looked at him, and you had to look back, because he had such a presence, he just exuded this personality."

Thompson was "amazing looking." More antique even than "Shakespearean," his was an Old Testament look, like Goliath in bronze armor or Ezekiel in a dusty sheepskin. He looked that way, and he was bigger and smarter and spoke in a lower register than almost anyone, and he could play the banjo like the devil himself. And none of that fully explains his singularity. The elegant lyrics of "Hot Buttered Rum"—a Thompson song I often hum or whistle—

capture the essence of the man I knew because they're both cynical and sentimental, side by side.

"It's always seemed to me a slight irony that a man of Tommy's breadth and genius didn't become very famous," said folklorist Henry Glassie. "I think he should have. Tommy wrote some of the finest songs of the genre of his period. In some ways, Tommy will probably be forgotten and his songs will be remembered."

It isn't that Thompson performed in obscurity or that show business disappointed him. From *Diamond Studs* off Broadway in 1975 to Broadway's *Fool Moon* in 1993, his credits for musical theater as an actor, musician, composer, and arranger would have made several careers for a less expansive talent. Two of the Ramblers' great supporters have been Sam Shepard and Garrison Keillor, and thanks to their patronage Tommy Thompson probably enjoyed more national exposure than any banjo player besides John Hartford. The Ramblers' music was featured on Keillor's *Prairie Home Companion,* in Shepard's film *Far North,* and on TV shows including *Northern Exposure* and *Ryan's Hope.* Thompson and company were the onstage band for Shepard's Broadway play *A Lie of the Mind,* and featured players in his motion picture *Silent Tongue.*

For a decade or more the Ramblers were in evidence everywhere, including Eastern Europe, the Middle East, and Africa, on tours sponsored by the U.S. Information Agency. But a dozen fine CDs made no one rich, and in the music business that's the single measure of celebrity. Thompson was a connoisseur's musician, a stylist who took on the mountain masters and won the World Champion Old Time Banjo Contest at Union Grove, North Carolina, in 1971. The Ramblers were a connoisseur's band, only with some wires loose. Their irreverent eclecticism—they all wrote songs in different styles—eventually moved them beyond the protection of every established genre.

What began as a traditional string band, rooted in mountain fiddle tunes and superb instrumentation—"a band that might have existed in 1930, but didn't"—evolved into an act that journalists struggled to describe. "A fantasy roadhouse band from a vanished rural America" was the *New York Times'* best effort. When Sam Shepard cast them as a raffish, impudent medicine-show band in *Silent Tongue,* it was less a performance than a Rambler self-portrait.

Even after Hollywood, Broadway, and the African odyssey ("Regions of Rain" is Tommy's ultimate road song), the Ramblers were proudly and thoroughly a local band. It was in Chapel Hill that they went to college or first met Father Banjo, resident master of the claw-hammer and the categorical imperative.

In Chapel Hill, the Ramblers and their faithful are not so much a cult as an extended family, with the closest family ties. A Ramblers concert was not an entertainment option but a seasonal celebration, like Mardi Gras or the Blessing of the Fleet in a fishing village. Everyone came—everyone with musical tastes to the populist side of Rachmaninoff—and everyone who could play wanted to play with the Ramblers. There were memorable nights when nearly everyone did. That atmosphere prevailed at Tommy's funeral. The service, a high-church Episcopalian affair with bells and incense, might have surprised the unchurched mountain Christian in the coffin. But upstairs in the parish hall afterwards, a dozen-deep string band—led by folklorist Alan Jabbour, the protean John McCutcheon, and original Ramblers Jim Watson and Bill Hicks—recreated the anarchic splendor of the vintage Ramblers when Father Banjo was in his prime.

Thompson was always the big man at the center, at the hammering heart of the music. How it must have stunned him, still in early middle age, when the music started to fade. But the performance I remember best created a quiet place where his deep voice cast a spell and his banjo rang pure as a church bell. *The Last Song of John Proffit,* a one-man show he wrote and created in its entirety, could stand as his own last will and testament.

His portrait of a nineteenth-century minstrel was a powerful piece of theater, charged with the passion and insight of a thoughtful man who'd been brooding and waiting a long time to take center stage in the spotlight, alone. Two St. Louis reviewers compared him to Mark Twain. Tommy was a riveting actor, with his stubborn streak of darkness and enough gravitas for the College of Cardinals.

And for once he was alone. Thompson's ego was so well tempered that he'd always worked with an ensemble—a formidable ensemble. Talent aside, if you've never seen core Ramblers Jack Herrick, Clay Buckner, and Chris Frank, well, they're not physical types you find every day in the coffee line at Starbucks. In such company, even Mount Thompson wasn't always the first thing to catch your eye. The Yoda-like Buckner, the most effortlessly funny man who ever made a fiddle cry, was responsible for "Father Banjo"—as in "Speak to us, Father Banjo. Read to us from the Book of Gigs."

Tommy wore his learning lightly, and covertly in the company of old-time pickers who entertain no excessive respect for books. He was alert to the condescension of people who take string-band musicians for grade-school dropouts, rarely yielding to the urge to embarrass them. He was easy in the most literate company. One of his best friends away from music was the Pulitzer Prize–winning poet Henry Taylor, whose intimidating erudition has shamed everyone who knows him, including me.

Taylor never scared Tommy. It was at the poet's house on the Outer Banks that we had—in retrospect—a first foreshadowing of the illness that was gathering its forces to bring the big man down. We'd been drinking a little. After dark six or seven of us walked out to the beach to look at the stars; one of my jokes was calling Tommy "Ursa Major." We took to singing, and after the amateurs exhausted their repertoire we turned to Tommy to keep us going—a man who in his time must have known a thousand songs. He sang one song, fumbled the lyrics of a second and then fell silent.

The evening was fairly young, and we thought it was just a mood, another cold front moving across his internal weather map. This was a year before the first symptoms of dementia were diagnosed. Tommy's last song that night wasn't one of his own—I never heard him sing his own songs in a social setting. It was one of his favorites, an ancient standard he sang in *John Proffit*: "Hard Times Come Again No More."

II. Spirits of the Place

The Last Autochthon

LISTENING TO THE LAND

Maybe John Barth wouldn't have said it in Mississippi. Key West is an offshore principality where "Southernmost" appears on scores of business signs, but where living thirteen hundred miles south of the Mason-Dixon Line means no more than it means in Havana. Surrounded by nomadic writers and professional exiles, the celebrated novelist from Maryland felt free to say: "Take England away from Henry James, and you still have a lot of James . . . but take Mississippi away from Faulkner and you've got a displaced person."

Maybe Barth meant no offense. But Southerners are prickly about Faulkner and fine-tuned to detect the faintest trace of condescension. Some remember that Allen Tate, in *The Profession of Letters in the South*, reckoned that the South "begins with southern Maryland"— good-bye then to Barth, H. L. Mencken, and the sins that stalk the streets of Baltimore.

Did this sly professor, this postmodernist quasi-Yankee, mean to imply that Faulkner's imagination, fastened organically to his "little postage-stamp of native soil," was in some way inferior to the one that fueled the effete and deracinated Henry James? The jab at Faulkner polarized Barth's audience, no less than his assertion that creative imagination dwarfs any feeble inspiration a writer may extract from his roots. Clouds of rhetoric parted, and a literary seminar called "The Spirit of Place"—on the face of it a lightning rod for clichés—had unexpectedly defined opposing camps with irreconcilable differences.

There are writers who believe that the physical earth is alive, pregnant with power and meaning, charged with suprahuman consciousness that shapes the imagination and underlies all literature. There are no mute places, they maintain, only deaf writers. (Montana's William Kittredge: "Stories help us find intimate imaginative connection with one another and the world—the environment, other creatures, and the biosphere, the living thing that we are a part of, without which we are nothing.")

To other writers, "nature" is a stony cipher, a blank slate on which human beings write well or poorly, and which only imagination can bring to life. "Without man, nature is barren," according to William Blake. The artist is Prospero, a sorcerer manipulating the elements, and nature is just a magician's assistant handing him his props. Art is eternal for these Platonists, and the material world is ephemeral.

Imagine two tribes who practice agriculture and hold it sacred, yet one worships the soil and the other worships the plow. These are two separate faiths, almost separate languages. A fraternity of distinguished authors, who had been feeling cozy and collegial, suddenly split in two and confronted each other across a gulf that would not be bridged in a weekend seminar, or in a lifetime.

When my own small role in the proceedings was concluded, my thoughts had turned to tennis and conch chowder. If I had slipped away, I'd have missed what became, on the Lilliputian battlefield of literary controversy, a clash of titans. At the aesthetic extreme sat John Barth, the apostle of artifice, the consummate literary gentleman without a trace of red clay clinging to his Foot-Joys. His company of geo-agnostics subscribed to Protagoras's declaration of primitive humanism: "Man is the measure of all things." In principle they agreed with Richard Ford: "Places have no spirit; sense of place is an invention, an artifice. What's important is happening in the foreground . . . it's what the people are doing."

On the other side of the table, crying "Hubris!" the druids of deep ecology held forth—writers like Peter Matthiessen and Barry Lopez, whose careers have been defined by epic journeys and reverent attention to a created world where man is a late and difficult arrival. To these pilgrims the environment is no metaphor, and aesthetic posturing in the face of geocide is repulsive.

"Many of you consider our species the rose on the dungheap of creation," said Matthiessen. "I don't see it that way."

"I know there are places of enormous power, for me," he said later. "And also places of negative power."

Even before Barth dragged Faulkner into it, the literary Southerner, like General Lee in the winter of 1860, could feel the wishbone pull of divided allegiance. Every Southern writer has felt the sting of the word "regional," implying that his proper and naturally inferior place was knee-deep in the moss-hung swamp from which he sprang. Each one stung has yearned to write a novel of manners set in Zurich or Bombay. Yet few Southerners are untouched by the autochthonous ideal—"autochthon" is that sinewy old word defined by Webster as "one held to have sprung from the ground he inhabits."

The Southland presses its ancient claims of land and blood. Alone among Americans, Southerners fought on their own land, were defeated, humiliated, and abandoned to it while the rest of the country transformed itself with commerce and waves of immigration. H. L. Mencken might have said that Southerners listened to the land— and, compulsively, to each others' voices—because culturally speaking there was no one else in the conversation. Heavily invested in the unchained imagination, today's Southern writer is nonetheless hesitant—nay, loath—to sell the farm and move to the postmodern suburb. The land, exhausted, may yet have something to say.

The autochthonous ideal has had its detractors. Its great bards and champions were the Nashville Agrarians; critics noted that they were teachers and intellectuals and no farmers at all. W. J. Cash, in *The Mind of the South*, argued that our agrarian myth was poisoned at its roots because slavery interposed itself between the Southerner and an honest relationship with his land.

In recent years the ideal has degenerated, in some quarters, into a competition for the humblest origins—who ate the most squirrels and chitlins, used the rankest outhouse, or grew up with the most lint in his hair. Writers whose parents were solvent or—God help them— educated have been sent to the back of the bus. I admire some of this "Rough South" literature, but when writers play the game of dueling hardships in public, it's hard to suppress a city-slicker snicker.

Like every endangered species, the autochthonous Southerner has suffered a devastating loss of habitat. The lines of communication between his land and his literature are breaking down. James Dickey is dead. The red-clay rumble (chthonic boom?) of his unshaven, un-manicured Rebel verse has scared its last Yankee. We've lost Eudora Welty, who wrote, "No matter how far you might range in fancy or imagination, I feel that your life line [in fiction] is connected to the real world around you." Gone too is Kentucky's James Still, author of *River of Earth,* who memorably wrote, "Being of these hills I cannot pass beyond."

Of living Southern-bred writers, the most critically acclaimed is Tennessee's Cormac McCarthy, who wants no part of "Southern" let-ters and, asked in my presence if he liked where he was living, replied "I never liked any place much." Richard Ford was born and raised in Mississippi but rejects a Southern label and relishes his role as a root-less blasphemer against The Spirit of Place.

If the South had its hundred years of solitude, they're behind us. Can any Southerner still speak for the earth in the old voice, the voice of Faulkner in "The Bear," of Robert Penn Warren in "Blackberry Winter"? If these hills are alive with stories, is someone listening?

The answer was in my mailbox when I returned from Florida—a new collection of the agrarian essays of Wendell Berry, *The Art of the Commonplace,* from Counterpoint Press. Berry is a living link be-tween Faulkner's earthbound old South and the writers who stood up for a sentient, embattled earth against Barth and his Platonists. Poet, farmer, novelist, essayist, Luddite, and polemicist, the archdruid from Henry County, Kentucky, is by his own account the Last Autochthon: "Within about four miles of Port Royal, on the upland and in the bottoms upriver, all my grandparents and great-grandparents lived and left such memories as their descendants have bothered to keep. . . . All that any of us know of ourselves is to be known in relation to this place . . . there is a sense in which my own life is inseparable from the history and the place."

The passage is from Berry's essay "A Native Hill," which could serve as Holy Writ for the Southern synod of the Church of Place. I'm not, myself, a deep-rooted man; I've never lived in a town where I had extended kin and family history. I was uncertain of my own place in this debate until I began to savor Berry. He may not be the last farmer-poet still working and reading his own land. But he's the writer—a fine, arguably a great writer—against whom any others will be measured. His prose, which never strays far from poetry, achieves casual epiphanies like this one: "My mind became the root of my life rather than its sublimation. I came to see myself as growing out of the earth like the other native animals and plants. I saw my body and my daily motions as brief coherences and articulations of the energy of the place, which would fall back into it like leaves in the autumn."

And again, from "A Native Hill": "To walk in the woods . . . mindful of its temporal extent, of the age of it, and of all that led up to the present life of it, and of all that may follow it, is to feel oneself a flea in the pelt of a great living thing, the discrepancy between its life and one's own so great that it cannot be imagined."

There are things that cannot be imagined, Mr. Barth. Imagination, wearing its other hats, has piped us to the edge of the abyss. Sometimes you have to shut down that gaudy machine, imagination—even one so gorgeous as yours—and simply listen.

He will not be immortal in words.
All his sentences serve an art of the commonplace,
to open the body of a woman or a field
to take him in. His words all turn to leaves, answering the sun
with mute quick reflections.
    —Wendell Berry, from "The Farmer, Speaking of Monuments"

The earth shall rise up where he lies
With steady reach, and permanent.
A shroud of cedars be his mound
This shield of hills his monument.

—James Still (1906–2001),

"Shield of Hills"

A Man of the World

In a country tribute to James Still's longevity, one of his neighbors told him, "You're the last possum up the tree." The last of his generation in Knott County, Kentucky, the neighbor meant to say. But Still, who died in April a few weeks short of his ninety-fifth birthday, was also the last of the undisputed "Greatest Generation" of American writers. William Faulkner, Ernest Hemingway, Robert Penn Warren, Thomas Wolfe, F. Scott Fitzgerald, Thornton Wilder, John Dos Passos, Allen Tate, and John Steinbeck were all born within a single decade at the turn of the last century, and it was their fiction and poetry that introduced most of the world's readers to the riches of American literature.

Still, born in 1906, was the youngest of these giants and the least celebrated. There are respectable readers, even English teachers, who fail to recognize his name. In contrast with the ceremonies for Eudora Welty, mourned like an empress last summer by Mississippi and the literate world, Still's wake was an Appalachian family affair. His limited renown, his admirers argue, was due entirely to regional prejudice and Still's reluctance to practice our culture-defining art of self-promotion.

"I think that up there in Knott County, well off the main track of the literary world, Still became a nearly perfect writer," wrote Wendell Berry. "His stories consist of one flawless sentence after another."

Such reckless praise invites a close reading of the venerable Sage of Hindman. Take the time. Though Still outlived all the rest, he was not prolific; his pursuit was perfection, not saturation. If you read the classic Appalachian novel *River of Earth* (Viking, 1940), the new collected poems (*From the Mountain, From the Valley,* University Press of Kentucky, 2001), and the 1977 story collection *Pattern of a Man* from Gnomon Press, you haven't covered James Still by a long shot but you've measured him fairly. If you're not impressed—if you're new to Still and you're not astonished—then possibly literature isn't your strong suit after all.

Acclaim has not been stingy. Poet Delmore Schwartz, hardly an Appalachian partisan, once called *River of Earth* "a symphony," and wrote of Still, "This man has something special." For his humanity and the psychological subtlety of his fiction, Still was described as an Appalachian Chekhov; for his populist humor with its marbling of black irony, he was compared with Mark Twain; in his fierce hermit's independence and minute observation of the natural world, he reminded readers of Henry David Thoreau. Stories like "Mrs. Razor," "Maybird Upshaw," and "A Master Time" are tone-perfect, simultaneously heart-vexing and hysterical, and so finely crafted that Wendell Berry rightly describes one as "almost a miracle." They'd have dazzled Mark Twain, or even the author of *Dubliners.*

Still's loyalty to the native dialect of Eastern Kentucky made him a hero in Appalachia but may have cost him the international reputation he deserved. His characters speak as their models spoke, in the speech of his neighbors on Troublesome Creek before the Second World War. To jaded urban ears a story in any regional dialect sounds like folklore, and critics and publishers are among the most jaded of urban animals. ("Thus an incoherent culture condescends to a coherent one," as Wendell Berry laments.)

Still himself was too quick to concede the point, once calling his stories "a social diagram of a folk society such as hardly exists today." But *Moby-Dick* is no less powerful because summer celebrities have replaced Nantucket whalers. *War and Peace* loses nothing human because Pierre's lost society of aristocrats lies buried under centuries of social upheaval and disaster. No "true" story, crafted by a writer of genius, ever becomes archaic.

James Still, a subsistence homesteader in a time before paved roads, a man who favored overalls and straw hats, claimed the label "hillbilly" never bothered him: "I count it as an honor, except when used as a slur." But before he settled in Knott County, he earned three university degrees, including a master's in English from Vanderbilt, where he was a contemporary of the famous Fugitive poets. Among his countless prizes and distinctions were two Guggenheim Fellowships; as a younger man he summered at the Yaddo and McDowell writers' colonies with most of the literary lions of his day. By standards far more cosmopolitan than Knott County's, he was a man of the world—a traveler who visited twenty-six countries and made fourteen trips to Central America to study Mayan culture.

But for most of seventy years you could find him in Hindman. When an artist of Still's stature lives so long in a place so remote he begins to draw pilgrims and generate myths, some of a quasi-saintly nature, like the story of the suit coat he left hanging on a bush for months because he refused to disturb a bird who'd built a nest in its sleeve.

Still loved the birds and beasts. But he was no St. Francis, no beaming haloed presence. He was proud, private, sometimes a little prickly. He could be flattered, but he wasn't one to roll over and wag his tail every time someone gushed, "I love your work." He could be distant, even impatient with academics, poetasters, and literary day-trippers. He preferred the company of children, animals, and writers—creatures without agendas, without *careers*.

"I've often remarked that he would be happy if there were only children in the world," said his friend Mike Mullins, director of the

Hindman Settlement School, where Still had served as genius loci since 1932.

"He's very innocent in a certain way," wrote my wife, Lee Smith, a writer with whom Still loved to flirt. "I don't mean to say he's childish. But there's a freshness and originality of language that I think is childlike. He has access to that part of himself that most of us have lost."

Not surprisingly, the narrator of *River of Earth* is a seven-year-old boy. At Still's funeral, one speaker revealed that "my dog Jack," immortalized in the poem "Those I Want in Heaven with Me, Should There Be Such a Place," was a dog the poet's father gave away when Still was seven years old—a wound he nursed for most of a century.

In his eighties and nineties, Still began to write for children, retelling—inimitably—Mother Goose rhymes and the "Jack" tales of Appalachian storytellers. When someone asked him why the dean of Appalachian literature was fooling with nursery rhymes, he replied, "I've been foolish the whole time." At the same time he was consuming literary magazines and journals; if you doubted that he kept abreast of the latest trends in fiction and poetry, he was always poised to set you straight.

Hillbilly intellectual, log-cabin hermit with a thousand luggage stickers, the oldest possum with the youngest heart—James Still sounds like a walking circus of contradictions. But contradictions trouble people who live and think inside the box; if Still ever knew the box existed, he never let on.

Conventional souls, often envious, call a man like James Still "a character." He wasn't an eccentric so much as a natural man who found a sanctuary where his idiosyncrasies were indulged. In Kentucky his world was subdivided by creeks and ridges, and among them he found all that he ever needed to write about. Despite his travels I've found only one published piece—a poem set in Belize on one of Still's Mayan expeditions—that didn't find its inspiration in Knott County.

At his memorial service one speaker after another tried to express how entertaining it was to know Mr. Still. (You called him "Mr." Still unless you were a writer he admired, a woman he fancied or his rare equal in years—a "Brother to Methuselum" like ancient Uncle Mize in one of his best stories.) They labored to capture his grand sense of mischief—his dark, deep-set eyes fairly glittered with it, right up to the end. They remembered him stretched out snoring on the reading table in the library, and his delight in smuggling six-packs and Kentucky Fried Chicken to the Trappist monks at Gethsemane Abbey, which housed that other garrulous hermit Thomas Merton.

It started me thinking about longevity. It's obvious that there are no special extensions for the pious or the virtuous, or the rich or wise either. Yet here was the oldest man for miles around, and by far the most interesting. Maybe Fate or The Reaper or whoever cuts our strings is actually a connoisseur like Scheherazade's sultan, and couldn't bear to interrupt Mr. Still in the middle of a wonderful story.

The most eloquent eulogist was Appalachian scholar Loyal Jones. To honor Still, Jones said, is to honor "art and integrity, and the need for some people to be different from the rest of us."

For me it was an august honor to do a couple of readings with him; I saved the programs. I excused his attentions to my wife because he was almost forty years older than we were, though no doubt I underestimated him. He was a strange and unforgettable man, and most people who knew him must have moments when he seems present yet. One morning I was reading Still's collected poems on a mountainside in North Carolina—a deliberate exercise, with one eye on the blue ridges and one hand on my dog.

I was deep in "Year of the Pigeons" when an emerald hummingbird descended on a flame-red phlox plant just six feet away. The poem and the bird struggled for my attention, until I imagined a voice I knew as well as the ageless face that I often studied on the sly. "Set that poem aside," it said, "and mind the hummingbird."

Among the True Believers

Waco, Texas, is a quiet respectable town, a city of 100,000 with a well-endowed university, several art museums, a zoo, a famous collection of the manuscripts of the nineteenth-century English poet Robert Browning. It welcomes visitors with tourist attractions as wholesome and nostalgic as the Dr. Pepper Museum and the Texas Ranger Museum. An 1870 suspension bridge across the Brazos River—once for cattle, now for pedestrians—links miles of parks and greenways. My 1950 edition of the Columbia Encyclopedia describes Waco's "air of ease and opulence."

It's a city of churches, of serious Christians. Baylor, the world's largest Baptist university, sets the moral tone for the town secular Texans call "the Buckle of the Bible Belt." But like its worldly neighbor Dallas, Waco is internationally famous for something it would rather bury and forget.

It was just eight years ago—after a fifty-one-day siege by the FBI—that the Branch Davidian compound near Waco was burned to the ground, killing eighty-five members of the cult along with its prophet, David Koresh. Today it's hard to find anyone in the city who cares to talk about the Davidians, and harder yet to get directions to the compound they called Mount Carmel.

But we hadn't journeyed to Waco, a place considerably off the beaten path, just to contemplate the wellsprings of Dr. Pepper or cruise the front gate of President Bush's ranch. By luck we met Tom, a photographer from Oregon. Discouraged by the townsfolk, he'd found his own way out to Mount Carmel, along the identical back roads and gravel byways of this flat, almost featureless countryside.

He drove us out there on a bright Sunday morning toward the end of a bitter Texas winter, a warm, cloudless day that belied the tornado watch we sweated all day Saturday (most of Waco was destroyed by a killer tornado in 1936). Instead of a burned-out hole in the ground, a site of desolation littered with glass and scorched timbers, we found a strange community assiduously rebuilding.

Mount Carmel has become a shrine to martyrs of the federal government's excesses, and as such it attracts like-minded pilgrims from all the millennial cults, armed posses, and Christian fringe sects that make America such a difficult place to govern or explain. When Janet Reno gave the order that triggered this massacre—or mass suicide or tragic accident, according to your prejudice—she provided a loose community of outcasts with an iron backbone of common grief and outrage.

Whatever happened here on April 19, 1993, the flames that were reflected in this quiet farm pond in a green meadow on the edge of the Texas outback are still burning bright, at least in the combustible imaginations of a host of passionate Americans.

The legions of the paranoid. Liberals call them "scary" but they aren't, unless you're so urban and sheltered that a few shoulder holsters set your knees to knocking. They have an Old Testament gravity about them, a way of looking you in the eye that says, "Ignore me at your peril." Several dozen came here on a Sunday morning, with their tools and picnic lunches, to finish the memorial chapel that stands on the slight rise above the cemetery where Koresh and the Davidians are buried.

Their children were running among the graves, each marked by a stone and a tree, now six or seven feet tall, that was planted in 1993.

The gravestones of the seventeen children who burned—"Star, 6," one is inscribed—are decorated with dolls, toy animals, a hobbyhorse. As an appeal to our sympathy the teddy bears may seem a little staged or obvious, but it's a hard-boiled visitor who doesn't pause and bite his lip.

"Where you from?" a gaunt, grizzled Jeremiah of a man asked my wife, and the answer, "North Carolina," apparently encouraged him to go on (I think "Chicago" might have stopped him).

"You ever use that sugar substitute they call Equal?" (She does, extravagantly, in the most alarmingly oversweetened tea and coffee I've ever gulped by accident.) "You do? Let me tell you, it's poison. It killed my wife, she got a brain tumor from drinking Diet Coke. Monsanto Chemical, they make it, those Bilderbergers, they hope you die. They belong to One World Order. It's an international conspiracy—businessmen who aim to reduce the population of the earth by 80 percent."

My wife was at a rare loss for words. Jeremiah made her write down the Web site addresses where she can get the rest of the story. He had just driven ten hours from Louisiana to help build this chapel and to meet other people who know about Monsanto.

A great deal of information is available at Mount Carmel. At the top of the driveway there's a bewildering display of millennial literature presented, we learned, by mainstream Davidians who reject Branch Davidians and declare Koresh a false prophet. Thirty feet away is the "official" information center, established by surviving followers of the martyred prophet. (Davidians are as prone to branching as their forerunners the Seventh-Day Adventists. Descended from followers of William Miller, who predicted the end of the world in 1843, Adventists sprang from one schism and produced several others before the turn of the twentieth century.)

Presiding over the official center—with photos of the apocalyptic fire and portraits of a beatific, guitar-playing David Koresh—was a woman in her eighties, of British origin, who believes she was divinely chosen to testify. She was in town visiting the sick, she said, when the FBI sealed off the compound. So, like Ishmael, she survived to tell the story of the doomed. Her allegiance is absolute, her memories more tender than bitter.

"It was wonderful then, with David," said the old woman in the stained camelhair overcoat. "All my life I had questions that no one could answer, no one till David. We're waiting for him to come back, you know. I search the faces of all the men who come in here, because you never know if he'll return in some disguise."

A leaflet contains one of the last epistles of David Koresh, in which he seems to speak directly for Almighty God:

"You're not rejecting a man by fighting against David my servant, no, for I have given and revealed my name to him. . . . Learn from David my seals or bear the consequences. I forewarn you, the Lake Waco area of Old Mount Carmel will be terribly shaken. The waters of the lake will be emptied through the broken dam. The heavens are calling you to judgment."

A dash of megalomania is an asset to a prophet, right up to the moment when the godless government rolls its tanks to his door. I was relieved that the ancient disciple didn't search my face for a moment, even, to see if I might be the next incarnation of her messiah.

These people aren't my people. I'm not given to high-octane, extraterrestrial religion, and I'm deaf to the siren song of guns, which brought the Davidians and so many other Americans to grief. Guns won't protect you from your government. There's no gun big enough, and arming yourself ostentatiously is one sure way to incur its wrath. Keeping track of extravagant concentrations of private firepower is one of the best things the feds do for us, as I see it.

The prophet's arsenal was his downfall. But a Sunday morning at Mount Carmel will shake your confidence that you know all about these people—or anything about them—from accounts in the media they detest. I came away with no conviction that they're insane, or acutely dangerous, just because "Get a rope" is their response when you mention Bill Clinton or either George Bush. There's a narrow path between gullibility and paranoia, and these are pilgrims who stray toward the far side.

Call them seekers with chronic compass problems. How many points are they off? David Koresh will not return—but neither, I suppose, will Jesus Christ. Monsanto may not conspire to kill us, but it likes us numbed and neutralized, and incurious about its business. Our government may not scheme to enslave us, but it loves a supine citizen who eats what's on the menu and believes what he sees on TV. Janet Reno may not be Satan's mistress, but she was ever a gutless and feckless public servant, and the teddy-bear cemetery at Mount Carmel is a ghastly memorial she could have avoided.

Branch Davidians insist that the Mount Carmel tragedy is analogous to China's pogrom against the Falun Gong. As we ratchet up the pressure to conform, to plug into the program and jump on the money train, we need to watch what happens to people on the stubborn fringe. Who's left, except six-gun Christians, to defend America's priceless heritage of privacy and self-reliance? Citizens who sleep well and see no evil always scared me more than insomniacs who see the devil behind every tree.

The flooded basement of the burned Mount Carmel compound is a reflecting pool now, and the sky it reflects is as calm and blue and nonjudgmental as an old Swede's eyes. A few miles away an elegant paneled library holds the elegant Victorian verse of Robert Browning, who wrote, "Ah, but a man's reach should exceed his grasp,/Or what's a heaven for?"

But I was standing on a basement wall near a burned-out school bus, reading " Eden to Eden" by David Koresh:

So Eve travailed and brought forth death
And passed the crown to all:
For each to learn the lesson here
The kingdom of the fall.

Storming Heaven

The old boys don't know what to make of Denise Giardina. When she announced her candidacy for governor of West Virginia, a bewildered Democratic functionary warned readers of one Charleston newspaper that there was "a darker quality" to her campaign, something "creepy" that made the hairs stand up along his spine.

West Virginia isn't the only state where populism has been buried so long its language frightens people. When Giardina talks about reversing ancient land grabs, when she challenges the prerogatives of coal and timber companies, she rings a bell that spooks every hack and time-server who stuffs his face at the public trough—a bell they haven't heard in those mountains since the days of John L. Lewis and Mother Jones.

The party drone who fears Giardina's "darker qualities" sees her through the lens of his own soiled conscience. Yet a dark side exists, one you couldn't overlook if you read her novels. The hero of *Storming Heaven*, based on the tragic Blair Mountain miner's rebellion of 1921, is a union organizer who loses his father and brother in a mine explosion. Subsequently all his friends are murdered by company thugs and he's gunned down in a final, futile battle against the coal companies and the U.S. Army. He dies, paralyzed, a few months later, and the book's last sentence reminds us that the companies—sixty-five years later—still own all the land.

Dark? It's a stroll in spring sunshine compared with Giardina's latest novel, *Saints and Villains*, a fictionalized biography of the martyred German theologian Dietrich Bonhoeffer. As a child during the First World War, Bonhoeffer lived near the Berlin Zoo, and one of his earliest memories was the screams of zoo animals slaughtered at night by starving Berliners. His short life encompassed the defeat and destruction of the first war, Germany's humiliation by the Allies, the rise of Hitler and the Nazi terror, the death camps and the Second World War. Arrested for his involvement in a plot to kill the Führer, Bonhoeffer spent two years in prisons including Buchenwald and was hanged from a spike in a prison yard in 1945, shortly before the final fall of the Reich.

As a writer Giardina seems drawn to these concentrations of soul-suffocating darkness. She has what those of us who share it call the tragic sense, the stoic's willingness to acknowledge that God's plan for the world, if He has a plan, has nothing to do with just deserts or happy endings.

"I'm not a rose-colored-glasses optimist," Giardina told the *Oxford American* in a classic understatement.

Sometimes the tragic sense can become a morbid obsession with disappointment and defeat. For Giardina, a seminary graduate and a lay preacher in the Episcopal Church, it functions as a spiritual challenge—another high bar to clear on the way to God. In *Saints and Villains* there's a passage from Bonhoeffer's journal that sums up Giardina's faith as I understand it: "But death cannot take us by surprise now, and we have seen enough of it to know that goodness and life can come from it. And it is after all better to die while living fully than in some trivial way. Something else we have learned that we might otherwise have missed. We have learned to view life from below, from the perspective of the outcast, the transgressors, the mistreated, the defenseless, the persecuted, the reviled."

In Giardina's fiction we find characters who announce that they aspire to sainthood, others who live as if they do. We find prisoners of conscience who refuse, repeatedly, to make their escape and leave others to suffer the consequences of fighting the powers that be. Giardina's people are passionate pilgrims who always come home, as she's come home to West Virginia. Her heroes are sacrificial figures— Christlike in their assumption of responsibility yet tragically human and vulnerable.

It's one thing to write it, another entirely to live it. Friends of Denise Giardina suspect that it's all the same to her, that the commitment she's made never ends on the printed page.

"She's the real thing, I think," said a friend, a fellow novelist. "She's as close to a saint as anyone you're likely to meet."

If you're put off by the sound of that, Giardina in person might change your mind. She wears her gravitas lightly. She's open, cheerful, unaffected, without a trace of vanity that shows on the surface. Irony is a language she can speak. The heightened sense of personal drama, a trait common to writers and politicians, appears to be missing entirely. And Giardina is heroically nonjudgmental. If you struck her as shallow and self-involved, she wouldn't condemn or even dislike you—she might pray, privately, for your improvement. It's her example, not her attitude, that tends to shame the frivolous.

Giardina is just a profoundly serious woman, in the antique mold of Mother Jones or Harriet Tubman. Incongruously, in an age of trivial grievances and whining victims' groups, she's here to remind us that serious politics are simple politics. They're about power, greed, and oppression and the underdog's eternal struggle for justice and dignity.

You've begun to suspect that I admire her. I recall only one time when I surrendered my sacred column space to another writer. That was in 1990 when I offered it to Denise Giardina to write about the Pittston coal strike in Southwestern Virginia, where she'd just been arrested, twice, for sitting in front of coal trucks that tried to cross a picket line. Her account of this classic coalfield confrontation —Pittston's president compared striking miners to Communists, Nazis, and the Ku Klux Klan—was so lucid and moving that for months

I was unable to write anything I thought my spoiled readers might regard as glib or facetious.

How does a woman of this caliber come to be running for governor, shoulder-deep in the chill murky waters of electoral politics? That same clueless Democratic hack suggested that Giardina is "on a power trip," drawn to the hustings by the familiar megalomania that motivates most of our political class.

This is no country for warrior saints, or even for soldiers of conscience. One fool's confusion about Giardina dramatizes the abyss that yawns between our cultural consensus and the exotic minority who live their lives according to fixed principles. A social conscience is treated like a social disease by media who make heroes of corporate predators and infantile celebrities.

They have no category that captures Giardina, a home girl from another moral galaxy. Yet people like her exist and persevere, usually in obscurity, even in America—priests of the church militant, outlaw environmentalists, social activists who work in migrant camps and abandoned ghettos.

Anyone familiar with Denise Giardina assumes that her quixotic campaign against mountain-leveling strip mines and the statehouse status quo is a form of ethical self-sacrifice. West Virginia is where her battle began and it's where she understands her mission to be. Like Dietrich Bonhoeffer, who fled sanctuary in England and the United States to return to Germany—in his case to almost certain death—Giardina would never forgive herself for escaping to a soft berth, teaching creative writing in Raleigh or Richmond.

She denies, of course, that it's painful to give up her writing and her privacy for a solid year of pressing flesh and talking policy: "No, really, I'm enjoying it," she told me, from a cell phone somewhere in the West Virginia panhandle. "There's so much to learn out here."

Giardina, who excoriated CBS for gullible promanagement coverage of the Pittston strike, claims that the media have been more than fair to her this time: "Maybe it's only because I'm a novelty and media feed on novelty, but we've had a lot of help getting our message out.

The issues we're pressing aren't exactly controversial. Anyone can see that the tops of our mountains are missing, and everyone knows who let it happen."

In a state with low voter turnout and widespread disaffection with King Coal and his Court of Democrats, Giardina sees herself as better than a long shot. She has a list of people she plans to hire if she wins. The Democratic monopoly may not be shaking in its coal-stained boots, but it went to court to try to keep her Mountain Party off the ballot, and it still refuses to include her in public debates.

It's uphill, but uphill is not a direction that fazes her: "If you do the right thing, something good comes of it," she said. "If I lose, well, I raised the issues and maybe I changed the nature of the debate. It takes time. It takes patience. Sometimes you look at history and it seems as if the bad guys always win.

"But if you look closely you see that some of the real bad guys lose in the end, and there's a human spirit that survives, that persists. Big coal has always won in West Virginia, but will it always win? I don't think so."

I asked her if she ever sensed a contradiction between the novelist's coal-black worldview and the reformer's resilient optimism. "It's a paradox, not a contradiction, and I like paradoxes," she replied. "It's a journey, the way I look at it. Let's see where it goes."

The Last Resort

It's a little after seven when I walk out on the balcony for my morning survey of the Gulf of Mexico. There are scattered clouds, a steady wind out of the northeast, and on the beach below me two street urchins, teenagers, doing what they so endearingly call "the wild thing" on our Smith and Hawken deck chair. On the striped cushions under the coconut palm they're fully dressed but fully engaged, managing nicely. Since they had climbed over an eight-foot fence or crawled through the surf under security wires to reach this love nest, it was no insignificant passion that brought them to our beach.

If it had been my front yard in North Carolina, I might have dialed 911 or at least yelled something sarcastic and discouraging ("May I bring you some coffee?") at these callow fornicators. But that's not the Key West way. A certain permissiveness, a hesitation to judge or censor your fellow sinners is part of making yourself comfortable here where the South ends and the United States of America never really found a foothold.

Flexibility is the only viable moral option in Key West, where some of the nicest people you'll meet smuggle marijuana. I overheard two grandfathers doing a domestic drug deal at a cocktail party. At Fantasy Fest, revelers wearing nothing but body paint stalk Duval

Street, which on New Year's Eve challenges Times Square with its own tradition, a drag queen named Sushi descending from Crabby Dick's balcony in a giant pink slipper. On every moonlit night, Cuban boat people stumble up on the beaches, gambling that these islands with too few rules will suit them better than an island with too many.

The most I can manage at the sight of the coupling campers is a heartfelt "Damn." But it's louder than I intend and they disengage, in no particular panic, and the boy helps his girl friend scramble over the wall. It gives us something to talk about at breakfast. Sex is the least of Key West's favorite mysteries; there's the sense here that unspeakable things are developing behind every garden fence. The middle-aged traveler feels a little younger, a little thinner and wilder just for walking by and listening.

They call it The Last Resort. Though it makes few demands on its residents or its visitors, there are caveats if Key West is a destination you're considering. If you like your egg the same way every morning, if you praise Holiday Inns because every room's identical, if your world is a geography of golf courses, stay away. If you're a homophobe or a cat-hater, if sloth and scruffiness and ambiguities disturb you, this is not the island of your dreams.

If you ask me why I repeatedly spend part of the winter in Key West, I don't have an easy answer. Does something much deeper than habit draw a reclusive, law-abiding, culturally conservative old gentleman to an island that's his opposite in every way? There are some relevant lines by W. H. Auden:

> Out of a Gothic north, the pallid children
> Of a potato, beer-or-whisky
> Guilt culture, we behave like our fathers and come
> Southward into a sunburnt otherwhere. . . .

"Otherwhere" is the wonderful word. I'd never argue that Key West has the best beaches, the best food, or the most remarkable tourist attractions. It may, however, have the best sunsets. Sunset is an elaborate ritual for Key Westers, celebrated every evening with an eccentric beggars' carnival—trained cats, an escape artist, a sword-swallower—on the wharf at Mallory Square. But the sky itself usually steals the show. The journals of John James Audubon, a visitor here in the 1830s, describe the pleasure of spectacular sunsets shared with friends. This year I witnessed a classic, a rare ring of bright clouds like the burly arms of Poseidon reaching toward the ocean, the sun a huge burning ruby cradled in his hands.

The island's elegance ends with its sunsets and the cream of its architecture. Like any winter resort, Key West includes the walled compounds and cool, tiled hotels of the very rich. But they don't set the tone or even noticeably alter it. Words like *raffish, jaded, louche,* even *unwholesome* come to mind when I think of this place.

The drugged and mad and muddled are prominent, sleeping on the sand, moaning in leafy corners. A stone's throw down the beach from our tasteful quarters is the notorious gay entertainment pier locals call "the Dick Dock," where the music is deafening and strobe lights reveal dirty dancing till long after midnight. Duval Street is a wasteland of predatory retailers, selling everything from sex—the Scrub Club massage parlor, the transvestite cabarets—to rubberized Key lime pies.

Key West's is a warped, elusive aesthetic, a siren song not every traveler can hear. A winter resident, a painter, helped me define it when he asked me if I ever planned to buy a house here, as he had. I didn't say so, but for me buying a house in Key West would be like building a hut at Machu Picchu—I love the view but I could never imagine being part of it. My attachment to the island begins with the fact that it's incurably exotic. It doesn't remind me of anything. You could call it home, it seems to me, only if home was a difficult concept for you, an issue. Except for the few Conchs—natives—whose ancestors crawled out of the channel or emerged from the mangroves two hundred years ago, everyone here is a visitor.

In my rented house I found Shirley Hazzard's reminiscence *(Greene on Capri)* of the quintessential traveler, novelist Graham Greene, one of the last of the haunted race of English nomads who fled, in the words of John Updike, "their wet, gray climate, their restrictive class system, their Victorian inhibitions, their Protestant work ethic with its grim Industrial Revolution."

"Even in a chosen setting, he retained the quality of wanderer," Hazzard says of Greene, and she quotes Malcolm Muggeridge: "Whatever his circumstances, Graham has the facility for seeming always to be in lodgings, and living from hand to mouth. Spiritually, and even physically, he is one of nature's displaced persons."

Nature's displaced persons come in different shapes and colorations. I'm not immune to the charm of family holidays, dogs by the fire, the myth of the rose-covered cottage where the wanderer comes to rest. On the other hand, I noticed early on that most people have one place they write and talk and reminisce about, while I always had many.

I never acknowledged—or needed or missed—one homeplace where I belonged entirely. I judge each place on its merits, and strangeness is a quality I prize. There are only a few places that seem to recognize the spiritually homeless and make them welcome. Key West is surely one of them. If we're displaced, then this must be a "dis-place," a non-place—a permanent outpost of The Otherwhere. Nature's DPs, her chronic travelers, are only at peace with the unfamiliar.

Authentic travelers gather here like migratory birds. A young American filmmaker, raised in Rome, confessed that to the best of his knowledge his parents own no furniture. Winter birds of Key West, they rent and make do from season to season, and always have.

Another itinerant Englishman, Cyril Connolly, wrote of "the brisker trajectory of the travel addict, trying not to find but to lose himself in the intoxication of motion." To understand him we need to distinguish between the traveler and his opposite, the tourist, who moves through exotic landscapes collecting snapshots and souvenirs, preferably in a herd of his own kind and loaded down with everything familiar he can carry, including his family.

Tourist money saved Key West, after the hurricane of 1935 washed away its railroad and the Great Depression put 85 percent of its residents on welfare. (In its nineteenth-century wreck-salvaging heyday,

Key West was Florida's largest city and the wealthiest community per capita in the United States.)

Bus tourists and cruise-ship lemmings throng Duval all winter. Nowhere in America is there a more existential interface—alien worlds touching briefly—than that Duval Street encounter between a blistered clueless tourist and a salt-cured, sun-dried old wino shrimper with the accusing eye of the Ancient Mariner, who looks as if nothing this side of hell could take him by surprise. But a block or two from Duval, it's as if tourists never existed.

Writers also come to the Keys; never Graham Greene, as far as I can figure, but Hemingway, Tennessee Williams, Wallace Stevens, James Merrill, scores of others. They're more prized here than in America, but like the rich and the tourists, they overestimate their impact on the ecology of this strange, slow place. I'm convinced that colonies of writers are on the whole a poor idea.

Don't come to Key West to meet writers. I come here to celebrate diversity, after my own fashion. I climb up to the observation deck on our rooftop, just before sunset, and survey a Scottish wedding on the hotel pier next door, a bagpiper playing "Amazing Grace." I can see the first lights on the shrimp fleet and on the Dick Dock, and a ravaged derelict sleeping something off on the Dog Beach next to Louie's restaurant.

An in-line skater glides up Waddell Street singing softly in Spanish, scattering feral cats. Around the hotel pool rich Europeans and Latinos air their tans and their sneers. In their midst, oblivious, a teenage boy with Down's syndrome repeats a yoga routine I seem to recognize as "Greeting the Rising Sun." The local paper reports two albino turkey vultures circling off Big Pine Key. I'm as far from home as I can go without a passport.

III. Portrait from Memory

A FINE DISREGARD

Though modern art has often dreamed of a closed society,

it can function only in an open one.

—Kirk Varnedoe, *A Fine Disregard: What Makes Modern Art*

A Prophet from Savannah

In college, most of us are too self-conscious and too anxious about our own uncertain fortunes to make accurate judgments of our peers. We're attracted to style without substance, often to individuals with neither if a deadly jump shot or a famous family is part of the package they present.

The hardest thing of all, when you're a boy—it was a single-sex New England college I attended—is to predict which of your contemporaries will become men who make genuine, lasting contributions to something greater than the alumni fund. Of the men I knew at Williams College, only two have been asked to come back and deliver the commencement address. One was a blowhard opportunist who achieved high office in Washington by endearing himself to right-wing politicians and financial success as the author of lowbrow bestsellers urging Americans to tone up their morals. Eventually he squandered most of his money and all of his political capital as a compulsive high-rolling gambler, the kind of megasucker casinos milk solicitously in private rooms.

The other commencement speaker was a much more interesting case. One Friday night in the fall of my junior year, I found myself—uncharacteristically—at a football pep rally with a towering bonfire and large posters foretelling the mayhem that the home eleven would soon inflict on Amherst. I noticed that the artwork on these posters was a great improvement over last year's and asked if anyone knew who the artist might have been.

"Sophomore named Varnedoe," someone replied. "He's a football player—lineman. A Southerner."

That was the first time I heard the name. On the Sunday after the last football game, while boys with thick necks and buzz cuts, liberated from training, stalked the campus in various stages of alcohol poisoning, I was in bed at noon trying to sleep through a certain hangover. There was a rough knock on the door, and two imposing figures hovered over my bed: the larger one was an ex-Marine noncom named Westy Saltonstall, and the other—I rubbed my eyes and reached for my bifocals—appeared to be wearing an entire suit, jacket and pants, of cotton printed with Budweiser labels.

"Crowther," croaked Saltonstall, "get dressed, you maggot, we're going to Cozy's. You know Kirk Varnedoe?"

Saltonstall, four beers into his Parris Island persona, was not a force I ever chose to resist. If not the biggest, he was surely the oldest man on campus, and his family had held half the first-class tickets on the Mayflower, or so we provincials believed. I pulled on my jeans while the kid in the Bud suit grinned at me. Did Kirk Varnedoe make a vivid first impression? Well, his suit did. Drinking was ritualized at Williams, to a degree that makes me cringe today. Drinking uniforms and accessories were not uncommon. One clown in KA wore a horned Viking helmet, like Hagar the Horrible in the comics; I myself owned a hard hat with my name stenciled on it, from a summer job in the steel mills. Even so, the Bud suit was a statement. I guess Kirk was saying, "I'm from Savannah, where people party seriously, whether you Yankees know it or not."

Those who dressed to drink often overplayed their roles, in my opinion, but this sophomore had a nice, recognizably Southern reserve about him. After all these years I thought I might have imagined the suit—a drinker's hallucination. But among Kirk's many obituaries last summer I found the same suit mentioned by Marcia Vetrocq, who knew him in graduate school at Stanford. I wonder who's wearing it now. It was a limited secret that Varnedoe, by Williams standards, was a drinker of no epic capacity who sometimes suffered grievously for weekend excesses. Another secret I can guess at, because it was my secret, too. The part of Williams we inhabited held hard work and serious study in serious contempt, so our academic enthusiasms and best grades remained carefully concealed from many of our friends.

Varnedoe must have been taking in something besides liquid calories at Williams, because six years later he had a Ph.D. in art history and was already an acknowledged expert on Rodin. He taught at Columbia and NYU and at thirty-eight won a MacArthur "genius" grant, an honor that at least symbolically left the rest of us far behind. At forty-two—a professor with no museum experience—he was named curator of painting and sculpture at the Museum of Modern Art. It was, and is, the most influential job in the fluid, insular, fiercely contentious world of modern art. Just two decades past his last Amherst game, the lineman from Savannah was sitting in the chair where the most critical decisions in his profession are made— "the conscientious, continuous, resolute distinction of quality from mediocrity," according to his Olympian predecessor, Alfred Barr. The Modern and its chief curator serve the American art establishment as a kind of aesthetic Supreme Court, and most of their rulings are beyond appeal.

This seat of power was the culmination of a spectacular rise, and Varnedoe gave every appearance of having been born for the job. With his rough-sketched Barrymore profile, his Low Country manners, and the Italian suits that somewhere replaced his Bud jacket—and his stylish, talented wife, the sculptor Elyn Zimmerman—he added a glamour that was brand new to the museum trade, and catnip to the celebrity-hungry tabloids that patrol Manhattan society.

Outside New York and the cloistered art world, the name Varnedoe might not be a household word. None of his eighteen books can be purchased in airports. But among artists and art professionals, his was a presence you could only compare to Tiger Woods or Russell Crowe. When he delivered the Mellon Lectures at the National Gallery in 2003, not long before he died, the museum was forced to rig extra auditoriums with audio relays. The lines wouldn't have been longer if Picasso had come back from the dead to sign autographs. Our Georgia boy was the closest thing to a rock star that art history has ever produced.

Marcia Vetrocq, his friend at Stanford, remembered him in just such an aura—"a motorcycle-riding rock star, impossibly handsome in a sea of sun-deprived academics."

"Unfortunately for us in the art world," Edward Goldman eulogized on NPR, "there is no heir apparent to his unique brand of magic."

We were all proud of Varnedoe, but of course we were amazed. Neither the talent nor the glamour had been readily apparent at school. His trademark rendition of the scabrous fifty-eight-verse rugby ballad "Eskimo Nell" provoked a near-incident on a flight to London, according to his teammates on the Williams College Rugby Club. They offered a consensus: "Anyone who knew Kirk in the sixties would find it hard to believe that he is now so well respected."

What do we remember? Obviously he was thoughtful, cut from different cloth than the guy with the Viking helmet. He'd give you this loopy grin, but if you paid attention you could see that something else was happening with his eyes. Alert, he was. Curious, aware. But an alpha intellectual and A-list celebrity, a sex symbol for the girls of Mensa? Come on. As his brother Sam said about the young Kirk in his eulogy, "The kid was bright, fun, and engaging, but he wasn't remarkable."

Some inevitable connection between the boy and the man has always been a leap of faith for biographers, a bridge of suggestion where insight and scholarship fail. Modern celebrity is much complicated by the media and the combustible cult of celebrity itself. "The spotlight hit the boy," Simon and Garfunkel sing—in another context—"and he flew away." Varnedoe was puzzled by his own image. You don't study art history to become rich and famous; it isn't like buying a guitar and a spangled body suit and driving to Nashville. Kirk had a comical response when the New York City gossip kittens labeled him "a hunk" and "a heartthrob." He looked in the mirror.

"If the definition of beauty is symmetry, this ain't it," he told his old Savannah friend Albert Scardino. "My face is skewed to the right because my jaw juts out one way and my forehead is out of balance and my ears don't match and I have all these moles all over the place."

The whole was more photogenic than the sum of its parts. But aside from the occasional photograph at a black-tie function, surrounded by famous faces, the man we knew at Williams seemed essentially unchanged (though his hair, by my rural standards, got a little too spiky for a while in the nineties). He was loyal to a fault. When he delivered the commencement address at Williams, he might have quoted Alfred Barr, Clement Greenberg, or some such oracle of modern art. Instead he quoted me, from a reactionary prodrinking essay, "The Night People," that I'd published in the *Williams Record* as my parting shot. When Varnedoe organized his first major exhibition at the Modern, the controversial "High and Low: Modern Art and Popular Culture," many art critics were brutally dismissive—but none of them noted that he'd commissioned the show's video guide from an old rugby buddy who was down on his luck.

He kept up with people, and if the old crowd never seemed to resent his conspicuous success—as they sometimes resented classmates who became corporate overlords—it was partly because he cut a prominent figure in a field they scarcely understood. For most of us, The Great Varnedoe was just an excellent adventure we could share vicariously.

This tendency to exempt him from envy was not shared by the art community, never known for its easygoing magnanimity. Kirk was a flashy, well-connected outsider who never earned his stripes in the curatorial boot camps, and the intramural sniping commenced even before he was installed at the Modern. One bone of fierce contention was an ad for Barney's men's store, photographed by Annie Leibovitz, with a mugging Varnedoe looking suave and surly in a suit by Ermene-gildo Zegna. A neglected footnote was that his modeling fee went to New York's Coalition for the Homeless.

By the time "High and Low" went up, in 1990, the wolves were circling and salivating.

"A textbook case for the maxim that an exhibition top-heavy in masterpieces can still be a disaster," sniffed Roberta Smith of the *New York Times*, a special enemy of the curator she chose to see, at the time, as a presumptuous South Georgia playboy. Varnedoe's retro-spectives for the Southern-born painters Cy Twombly (1994) and Jas-per Johns (1996) were more successful with the highbrow critics. But the ad hominem backbiting never truly abated until the announce-ment in 1996 that he was being treated for advanced colon cancer.

That's New York for you. According to Robert Storr, his colleague at the Modern, Varnedoe was "clearly wounded by the intemperate nature of some of the attacks." If so, they weren't wounds he licked in public. We'd been out of touch after I left New York—though he kept sending me invitations to openings—but I began to see Kirk more often in the nineties. The meanness he had provoked was a mystery to me, just as it was a mystery why all other museum curators were invisible scholars and Kirk was like Sky Masterson in *Guys and Dolls*. It was in 1998, when he had apparently recovered from his cancer, that I finally began to understand what the boy in the Bud suit had made of himself and why I should pay attention.

He had just opened his Jackson Pollock retrospective to wide ac-claim. He invited a few of his Williams friends to tour the exhibition at eight in the morning, before the museum opened, and educated us painting by painting as we walked through it with our wives. In all honesty, I'd never been a Pollock enthusiast. English majors, with their weakness for narrative structure, are resistant to abstract ex-pressionism, and Pollock's neurotic chaos is especially intimidating.

After an hour of looking at Pollock's paintings through Varnedoe's eyes, I saw Pollock as I'd never seen him before. More dramatically, I saw Kirk Varnedoe as I'd never seen him before. Varnedoe at fifty was a spellbinder, as they used to call them, who could have sold Pollock to a Pre-Raphaelite or Andy Warhol soup cans to Cosimo de Medici.

It's hard to admit that someone you knew as a teenager is a genius of any kind. Yet here was a pure genius of the lectern at the top of his form. It was a rare privilege to watch him work with the paintings themselves. At the Mellon Lectures last year I learned that he was just as good with a carousel of slides—a magician, like Ricky Jay with a deck of playing cards. He could dazzle and hypnotize. When I asked him for the text of his Mellon lectures, he explained—with mixed pride and sheepishness—that he never lectured from a text, or even from notes. The same memory that conquered the formidable "Eskimo Nell" had somehow absorbed the entire chronicle and spectacle of modern art.

"Preacherly" was a word someone used to describe him at the podium. "Art is my religion," he told TV's Charlie Rose. And I recalled the classroom style of Lane Faison, Kirk's mentor, the legendary Williams art professor—still lecturing at ninety-seven—whose students now run about half of America's major museums. Faison, also a maestro of the slide projector, approached the study of art as if it were some vigorous outdoor sport, some voyage of discovery for hardy bronzed sailors, not "sun-deprived academics."

"For Lane, art was very much a personal experience," Varnedoe said once. "It was between you and the object."

Varnedoe was Faison's perfect disciple. "For Kirk, art was as physical and pleasurable as being knocked down by a wave," said his former student, *New Yorker* critic Adam Gopnik. Artist Chuck Close praised "his passion for objects over ideas." From his ideal perch at the Modern, Varnedoe became prophet, high priest and principal evangelist for his own cult of strenuous engagement, his church for aestho-athletes driven to probe and pierce and wrestle with works of art until they yielded their secrets. If art can spawn fauvism, Dadaism and the Ashcan School, why hesitate to coin a name for Varnedoe's faith? "Sinewism" seems to work. My coinage may not catch on with the art historians, but brief research reveals that Kirk loved the word "sinew" and used it: in Giacometti's sculptures he found "the resilient sinews of humanity."

Genius and hard work notwithstanding—friends say he worked eighteen-hour days—it was a miracle of good fortune for Varnedoe to win the one job on the planet where his gifts and passions could make the biggest difference. Such favors are rarely granted by the gods, and the gods never fail to exact a price. Varnedoe spent fourteen years at the Modern, nearly half of them in the shadow of a life-threatening illness. The cancer recurred in 2001 and eventually metastasized. As treatments began to fail him, Kirk put the last of his strength into his Mellon Lectures—a six-part, nine-hour defense of abstract art titled "Pictures of Nothing," which became one of those triumphs of will and spirit that eyewitnesses make into stories to tell their children. His final lecture was an eloquent, prophetic flight of free association. None of us who were there, not even those few who raised a glass with him afterwards, could point to any sign that this was not a man at the peak of his powers. Less than three months later he was dead, at fifty-seven.

"To the last, Kirk considered himself to be a lucky man," wrote Marcia Vetrocq, echoing the last public words of a New York idol of another era, the great Lou Gehrig, dying of MLS: "I consider myself the luckiest man on the face of the earth."

Gehrig was another big, good-looking jock who in his life was dealt many good hands and one very bad one. Varnedoe chose to introduce his final lecture with the less-quoted last words of the android Roy Batty (Rutger Hauer) in Ridley Scott's film *Blade Runner:* "I've seen things you people wouldn't believe—attack ships on fire off the shoulder of Orion, bright as magnesium; I rode on the back decks of a blinker and watched C-beams glitter in the dark near the Tannhauser Gate. All those moments will be lost in time, like tears in the rain. Time to die."

A certain percentage of the overflow audience understood that Varnedoe was dying, and at these words, of course, that percentage was in tears.

"There it is," Kirk concluded when his last slide faded from the screen. "I have shown it to you. It has been done. It is being done. And because it can be done, it will be done. And now I am done."

I never saw him again, after that astonishing Sunday at the National Gallery. The apostle of Sinewism had issued his last encyclical. But once you've heard a great preacher, you're bound to sample his version of the gospel. Varnedoe's books and essays have been as much of a revelation to me as his virtuosity in the pulpit. We assign the highest intelligence to those who agree with us, and without ever discussing anything philosophical—sports and friends, and maybe France, made up the whole of our conversations—this brilliant Varnedoe and I had arrived at many of the same conclusions.

He used his influence to oppose the dreary, reductive Marxism and Marx-inflected theory that casts us all, even artists, as helpless prisoners of our own narrow context. Everything an artist creates is predictable, according to these grim antihumanist heretics, if we can fix him within the correct contextual coordinates. To these theorists art is an incidental byproduct of the class struggle, and genius, inspiration, even talent and quality are decadent, repressive elitist notions.

Anyone who ever loved art or literature believes intuitively that this is philistine rubbish, that it's always what *can't* be predicted, what's individual and eccentric—the sudden insight, the rogue notion—that lights up the canvas, the page, and the world. Against reductive theory, Varnedoe declared his belief in "the individual human consciousness, for all its flaws and deforming optics, as our prime resource and treasure." The title of his most definitive book on modern art, *A Fine Disregard,* comes from the story that rugby was invented when an English soccer player, displaying what his commemorative plaque calls "a fine disregard for the rules," suddenly picked up the ball and ran with it.

Varnedoe scorned inevitability and worshiped the random. As a literary critic, I declared the same faith and fought the same fight against the same ferocious philistines. Somehow we belonged to the same church, Varnedoe and I. Was there any significance in the fact, confirmed after Kirk's death by his brother Sam, that we both carried not-so-secret torches for Emmylou Harris? (He also loved Elvis and Sam Cooke.) The novelist Kurt Vonnegut, with whom Kirk was occasionally confused, invented the concept of the karass, a group of people with something important but subtle in common. Opposed to the karass was the granfalloon, a group with something utterly superficial in common—like Williams College alumni.

Often as not, what intrigued Varnedoe intrigues me. Especially the book he never wrote but mentioned in every interview—his book on "how Rauschenberg, Johns and Twombly, three Southern boys, changed the world." In the near-century since H. L. Mencken dismissed the South as "the Sahara of the Bozart," Southern artists have struggled to be taken seriously by the New York mandarins, or even by their own regional museums. It was no coincidence that Varnedoe, a Southerner unexpectedly appointed chief mandarin, devoted two of his major retrospectives to Johns and Twombly. As loyal to his roots as to his friends, he had big plans for the South's undernourished reputation, but he ran out of time.

Since the fifties, modern art has revered Johns, from South Carolina, and Robert Rauschenberg from Port Arthur, Texas. Varnedoe's warm endorsement helped elevate Twombly, from Lexington, Virginia, to nearly the same level. The problem is that these artists have lived and worked chiefly in Italy or downtown Manhattan, and that their work—abstract, runic, cerebral—betrays little Southern influence to the layman's naked eye. Good old boys they are not.

Varnedoe's eye, of course, was no layman's, and the Southern accents in his own work are never hard to find. His simile for Alberto Giacometti's irony—"as earthy as the slouch of a loping hound"—leaves me grinning conspiratorially. Only a Southerner with Kirk's discernment, eloquence, and tenacity could ever have sold this worldly trio back to the home folks, or sold them to anyone as Dixie's darlings. He's on record with a theory about Twombly—that Civil War–saturated Lexington, with its monuments and sites sacred to

Lee and Stonewall Jackson, had turned the artist toward military mythology and paintings like his series "Fifty Days at Ilium." No one questions that armed ghosts haunt the South. Jasper Johns took his first name from a Revolutionary War hero, Sgt. William Jasper, whose statue stands in a Savannah square. Johns painted American flags and maps of America, and his stepfather was named Robert E. Lee. But that's pretty thin, and Rauschenberg's Southern echoes seem thinner.

Varnedoe's last e-mail, a week before his death, promised me a couple of sentences of insight into this pet project. They never came, of course, and I've been looking for clues ever since. Most helpful was another of his former students, Jeffrey Weiss, curator of modern art at the National Gallery. Weiss said that Kirk had spoken of "a shared language" of art that the three artists developed (they worked, lived, and sometimes slept together in several combinations), a language based in part on their shared experience of Southern culture.

Even the most illustrious career leaves much undone, much unsaid. Taking advantage of the unrestrained hospitality of Varnedoe's sister Comer Meadows, I made a respectful pilgrimage to Savannah. Touring the famous squares, I encountered Sergeant Jasper and a dozen houses connected to Kirk's family, branches of which have been prominent in the city for centuries. I stayed in the rambling beach cottage on Tybee Island, I ate oysters with Kirk's brother Gordon at the Crab Shack. I walked through the ancestral hunting cabin, now decomposing in the pinewoods. I saw the big brick house on the square where he grew up, and portraits of Johnny Unitas and Ray Charles he drew when he was a boy. We stood on the bluff where a few bricks remain of the family's last "big house," Beaulieu, which burned in 2001.

And finally, the Varnedoe grave sites, under a huge live oak smothered in Spanish moss, on a bluff overlooking the river and the salt marshes. Deep South with all the trimmings—scenes from *Midnight in the Garden of Good and Evil* were filmed just down the river. Several graves are flying Confederate battle flags, and nearby is a headstone for Kirk's cousin, Braxton Bragg Comer.

The footprints end there, light-years from that museum on Fifty-Third Street in Manhattan. All in all, a Southerner's life that showed a fine disregard for the rules, and managed to change a few. Maybe it's not too grand to recycle Jasper Johns's epitaph for Marcel Duchamp: "He has changed the condition of being here."

IV. Objections Sustained

A Farewell to Arms

The rising sun is just clearing the ridge behind me, lighting up weeping cherry trees in peerless full bloom. A fresh breeze carries the dense sweet scent of wisteria down the terraces to the bench where I read my newspaper. So far I'm the only Sunday pilgrim in the Sarah P. Duke Gardens—which every April make their powerful plea for the tarnished soul of old Buck Duke, the tobacco baron whose vast bloody fortune built the university, the hospital, and the chapel that tower over this vernal splendor.

It's the first morning of daylight saving, the first Sunday and first clear perfect day of the cruellest month, and here in the Eden that Buck built, it will be a blessed hour before tourists and photographers begin to cluster around the koi pond and the weeping cherries. I'm acutely aware of my good fortune. In Iraq, friends and former colleagues are chewing sand and ducking bullets in one-hundred-degree temperatures. Tomorrow morning, one of them will dominate the obituary page of the *New York Times*. But it's the local paper that I'm reading, and I see that the second headline—after "Siege of Baghdad Begins"—honors a local Marine, Lance Corporal Brian Anderson, killed Wednesday in the desert west of Masiriyah.

"Marine 'gave his life for the rest of us,'" it reads, quoting Corporal Anderson's mother. This wasn't a classic death like the ones Marines die in John Wayne movies, cut down in firefights against impossible odds. The corporal, operating a .50-caliber machine gun atop a seven-ton truck, was electrocuted when the truck rolled through some low-hanging power lines.

Anderson was born and raised here in Durham. Though he lived within a mile of campus, the cloistered, expensive world of Duke University would have been as remote from his experience as Baghdad. He played football, ran track, and wrestled at Riverside High School, sang in the choir and played conga drums at Mount Calvary United Church of Christ. He enlisted in the Marines shortly after his high school graduation in 1996, "probably trying to find himself," said a family friend.

According to his mother, Anderson planned to reenlist next December and was hoping to learn computers. His friends described him as popular and easygoing, his potential beyond the Marine Corps largely unexplored. His official photograph in the Corps' striking dress uniform suggests a confident young man who had found a home and a focus at Camp Lejeune.

Anderson's is a representative portrait from the professional, all-volunteer armed forces that are fighting America's wars—and a fairly typical profile of the Southern warrior, circa 2003. It's here in the South, particularly in North Carolina with its sprawling bases and military economy, that virtually any war is embraced with enthusiasm. If the president declared war on Quebec—even on South Carolina—he could expect Tar Heels to give him the same 75 percent approval that greeted his "liberation" of Iraq.

If you've never seen a three-year-old dressed in camo and a Special Forces beret, try a gun show in Raleigh. Ours is a martial province, bounded on the south by Georgia, where they're still hammering out a compromise on the Confederate battle flag, on the north by Virginia, where Richmond troglodytes are fighting a rearguard action against Daniel Frech's statue of Abraham Lincoln. Liberals who like the cut of North Carolina's ambitious senior senator, John Edwards, are stunned to discover that he's a firm supporter of the Baghdad adventure. They don't understand that any other position would eliminate his political influence in North Carolina forever.

Among Tar Heels, "supporting the troops" seems to mean a good deal more than praying for their safe return. Very little changes here, from war to war—except the young people in uniform, and the families that produce them. It's a substantial irony, lost on many "supporters" of the late Corporal Anderson, that Abraham Lincoln's war won Anderson and other African Americans their right to wear the gorgeous dress uniform of the United States Marines. There are star-spangled, pennant-waving white people here and elsewhere whose passions for the armed forces and for college basketball—roughly equal—are untempered by the fact that their own children no longer participate.

Just as coaches at the South's mostly white universities earn millions exploiting black players from urban ghettos, white generals from West Point earn their stars on the backs of men like Brian Anderson. As an athlete he wasn't good enough for Duke, for the crosstown bus ride to glory that was the impossible dream of every kid in his neighborhood. But he was good enough for the Marines, good enough to fight in the desert and die in one of the most dubious wars Americans have ever tried to justify.

A volunteer army is a poor people's army. Anderson was a child of privilege compared to Lance Corporal Jose Gutierrez, another Marine who died in combat south of Baghdad. Gutierrez was an orphan from Guatemala who crossed the Mexican-American border illegally at fourteen. He joined the Marine Corps as an immigrant foreign national, but through the infinite generosity of the immigration bureau, he was naturalized posthumously and buried as a United States citizen.

Casualty reports, like Division I basketball teams, rarely include middle-class white kids anymore—a fact legions of war lovers have agreed to ignore. Avoiding military service is as easy as getting into college, and these days that's a pretty low hurdle to clear. This class exemption is hard to take when it's personified by smug sophomores whose exposure to violence consists of fraternity hazing and posttournament riots. It's impossible to take when they express enthusiasm for wars of Arab liberation. A friend of mine, a professor at Wake Forest, had one student who objected strenuously to antiwar sentiments she expressed in class. "I respect your right to choose," she told him. "I guess this means you'll drop out of school and enlist." As she tells it, the war weasel recoiled as if he'd been stung by a hornet.

Iraq is a surrogate's war fought by the children of an economic underclass, a remote war compared to a struggle for national survival like World War II, when Rose Kennedy's sons took the same risks as her chauffeur. A cynical war of geopolitical chess, it seems unworthy of patriotic posturing. (If you want to keep the enemy in check, Henry Kissinger would say, you have to sacrifice a few pawns.) This is a war in which only the most hypocritical propagandist—or the most heartbroken mother—could claim that a fallen Marine "gave his life for the rest of us." Yet the life he gave is no less precious, whether the Marine's enemy is Adolf Hitler or some grotesque, well-oiled dictator who fell out with old friends in the U.S. State Department. In a time of sordid little wars with suspicious agendas, how does the martial South keep faith with its warriors?

Do we call Corporal Anderson a hero, a martyr, an innocent victim? On the surface he was just a young man in search of direction, self-discipline, and self-respect. The Marine Corps is the last place I would have looked for them myself—if you remember the fat, humiliated recruit in Stanley Kubrick's *Full Metal Jacket,* the one who ultimately kills his drill instructor and himself, he's the character in war films with whom I most closely identify. But I've known too many Marines to doubt that the Corps delivers most of what it promises in the line of pride and self-respect. Right up to the instant when he hit the power lines, Anderson must have thought he'd struck a fine bargain with the U.S. Marines.

It's fraught with such complexity, this business of "supporting our troops." Antiwar extremists made a fatal error when they stigmatized soldiers for the debacle in Vietnam—an error that never tempted me because my brother was serving in a forward unit. But consider the current right-wing rhetoric, insisting that a patriot drops every objection to military action once U.S. forces are committed. This is moral quicksand, a mindless lemming-rush to moral suicide. Followed to its logical conclusion, it outlaws individual conscience and mandates unanimous civilian support for every bellicose tyrant from Hitler to Idi Amin—or Saddam Hussein.

We honor our soldiers by separating the reasons they're in Iraq—because military risk falls unequally on minorities and the poor, because U.S. foreign policy is turning toxic, because a paranoid America is turning mean and ugly since 9-11-01—from the irreducible fact that they are there, where we have no right to send them unless we'd gladly fight alongside them. Corporal Anderson was there, and his Durham neighbors in the Duke-blue sweaters were not. I can call him a hero, not because he died defending American ideals—he died obeying masters who flout them—but because he died defending his fellow Marines, exposed in a conflict they did not cause or seek.

The face of war has changed immeasurably since Lee and Longstreet sat by their campfire at Gettysburg; war as it touches individuals is always the same. Pure pacifists say we must never praise soldiers, because the wars will never end until all the world's young men (and now women) refuse to serve. Until then—until, perhaps, the end of time—we rely on Corporal Anderson. I don't feel compromised, as an incorrigible war-hater, when I say that I'm proud of him. I'm equally proud of the ragged band of war protesters I met last week at the University of Virginia, marching soaked in freezing rain, herded by contemptuous police, carrying the homemade banner "Regime Change Begins at Home." Like mine, their support for Corporal Anderson consisted of fervent, unanswered prayers for his safe return. Though gulfs of circumstance and misunderstanding still separate them, it's a noble dream that someday the warriors of conscience and the warriors of necessity will march on common ground.

The Old Dragons Sleep

Through a harsh winter of saber-rattling anxiety, there was almost no good news for America except the final farewells of Jesse Helms and Strom Thurmond, Jim Crow's last prominent disciples, Carolina's last living (barely) monuments to segregation and white supremacy. Followed directly by Trent Lott's farewell to power, the old dragons' departure was a small island of hope in a wintry sea of cultural desolation and political regression.

The good news for the South is that the last politicians directly implicated in its ancestral sin have been mothballed. Even in extremest senectitude, Helms and Thurmond were the twin towers of Southern reaction, in whose knobby old shadows toxic strains of Confederate nostalgia still bloomed unchecked. A giddy outburst of that nostalgia sealed the fate of their unctuous protégé Senator Lott, who was abandoned by the White House and eaten alive by the national media. The irony is that Lott's rise to majority leader has been a triumph of media narcolepsy and Republican hypocrisy.

"Recent comments by Sen. Lott do not reflect the spirit of our country," said President Bush, who knows that without George Wallace in 1968, without the cynical, racist-soothing Southern strategy Wallace inspired, no Republican except Eisenhower would have been elected president in the past seventy years.

Trent Lott's ragged résumé was no secret. Republicans knew exactly what they were getting when they came courting Southerners in the seventies. They were getting the worst of us, and they got plenty— Klansmen, white citizens' councils, Dixiecrat demagogues, sullen race-baiting reactionaries who had been a chronic embarrassment to the national Democrats. Come to think of it, unless your civil rights credentials are impeccable—unless you marched with Martin, at least—a Southern conservative is a morally indefensible thing to be.

It was never a question of whether most Republicans agreed with these Neanderthals. As a minority with an aging, dwindling, monochromatic core of true believers, the Republican Party could not survive without them. It was always a neat trick to feed the fires of racial resentment with one hand and wave the torch of equality with the other, and it fooled most of the press most of the time.

It never fooled black voters. A quote I treasure is attributed to J. C. "Buddy" Watts, Sr., whose son J. C. Junior recently gave up his seat as the lone black Republican in the U.S. Congress. "A black man voting for the Republicans," said Buddy, "makes about as much sense as a chicken voting for Colonel Sanders."

The quick clean castration of Senator Lott delighted Southern liberals, black and white; it gave punch-drunk Democrats a rare taste of blood that was not their own. But for the South there was no net gain in this ritual humiliation of one Mississippi mossback. In Manhattan, no one would have blinked if Lott's wardrobe had yielded a hooded Klan robe. They honestly believe that half of us have one hanging somewhere—not freshly pressed for a rally, necessarily, but at least in the back of the closet, where a man of fashion might hang his old white dinner jacket just in case.

I wish I were exaggerating. I'll bet—though not the ranch—that Trent Lott never owned a hood. What the reporters pulled out of Lott's closet was his mean old racist mama, Miss Iona, who once wrote the integrationist editor of the Pascagoula paper, "I hope you not only get a hole through your office door but through your stupid head."

Against a mama like Iona, you'd need at least a Senate seat before you could hold your own. Miss Iona, a schoolteacher, was just what knee-jerk New Yorkers needed to renew their Mississippi stereotypes for another fifty years.

Change is dramatic in the modern South but very, very recent. You could still fill every seat in Yankee Stadium with fierce old ladies like Mrs. Lott, without beginning to empty the rest homes of Mississippi. The sons they raised know that a racist heritage dies hard. A few Mississippians, like the Greenville editor Hodding Carter, committed their lives to overcoming and overcompensating for it. Trent Lott spent his life exploiting it where he could and hiding it where he couldn't.

Sympathy for the senator is more than I can manage. But there's another Southerner who knows how much can be lost, and how suddenly, when the sky turns black with the circling buzzards of the necrophagic press. And I can't object when Bill Clinton describes Lott as a hapless scapegoat, an unpopular party soldier diced into buzzard bait to distract us from the actual scandal, the two-faced racial policy that created a Republican South.

I deplore public burnings by the speech police. I remember a South Georgia boy, John Rocker, a dumb relief pitcher who was crucified for blithering over a beer. But this Lott affair reveals the careful choreography of a ritual sacrifice. Editorialists took a few weak swings at Strom Thurmond, no doubt assuming that he's too deep in the shadows to take offense. But during the lynching of Senator Lott there was almost no mention of Jesse Helms. Was Jesse protected by some kind of geriatric amnesty, the same courtesy that tried to whitewash the doddering Richard Nixon, a president who called people "little kikes" on tapes he intended for posterity?

"To many of us, Jesse Helms is a hero of almost mythic proportions," Trent Lott rhapsodized at Jesse's official Senate farewell. "Jesse Helms transcends his times. He is the senator's senator."

Good grief. At times we must suspend our obligation to speak well of the decrepit and the dead. I've been listening to Jesse Helms and recording his transgressions for most of my adult life. He is, to the best of my knowledge, the only diehard segregationist who never apologized or made any effort to atone. Even George Wallace apologized.

I allow that Helms gave good constituent service and that he attends the ladies with the courtesy of an antebellum gentleman. We might have settled for less service and worse manners from our senator. While Helms represented North Carolina, he also represented segregation, regression, repression, homophobia, McCarthyism, mill bosses, and big tobacco. When Hendrik Verwoerd and South African apartheid had just one friend left in Washington, it was Jesse Helms. His office was the North American consulate for the fascist dictators and death squads of Latin America. His apoplectic, comical anticommunism was all of a piece with his racial blindness. I think it was Hodding Carter who said that, for people like Jesse, "communists were Negroes who wanted to vote and white people who thought they ought to."

Helms must have invented the clumsy code that politicians like Lott use to reassure racists of their sympathy. When the N-word became unacceptable, they honored Jim Crow's memory by opposing the Martin Luther King holiday and the Voting Rights Act, defending the Confederate battle flag and railing against "outside agitators" and (my favorite) "secular humanists." Toward the end it was easier for Jesse to focus his attacks on homosexuals, with the understanding that the great gay conspiracy implicated all his other enemies as well.

He was not a smart man, our Jesse. He was an anachronism by definition—Jim Crow and the Cold War were the frozen polestars of his life. He stood for everything ancient, ugly, and encrusted with ignorance that shames the South. George McGovern once described Helms off the record (and then told me, "No, leave it on") as the man who'd done more than anyone in history to impede the effectiveness and damage the credibility of the United States Senate.

"When Helms goes, something goes out of the Senate that we won't see again," orated Sen. Robert Byrd, and to that we add a fervent "Thank God."

But Jesse, too, had a mama and a papa, and a hometown and a moment in history that formed him. His father, Big Jesse, was a policeman whose idea of keeping the peace was to prowl the streets of Monroe, North Carolina, with a baseball bat, making African Americans feel endangered. In 1958, Monroe was the scene for one of the most incredible racist outrages since the lynch mobs disbanded. A nine-year-old boy, Hanover Thompson, was convicted and sentenced to fourteen years in prison for attempted rape—because a little white girl kissed him on the cheek. (North Carolina courts rejected his appeals, but a national outcry freed him.)

If the Helms family left any fingerprints on that atrocity, I don't have the story. But with neighbors like these, what were the chances that Jesse would grow up to be John Brown, or even George McGovern?

The South can't afford to forget, conceal, or make excuses for these travesties—what excuse applies?—but we have to place them in the realistic context that moral absolutists abhor. Asking a white man raised in Mississippi or Monroe why color is so hard to ignore, that's like asking black Southerners raised in poverty why so few of them own banks. Because the old race dragons—fear, guilt, rage—have been coiled in the hearts of Dixie so long they hold the mortgage, and it takes generations to buy them out. "Organic" is the word W. J. Cash used to describe the tragic, intimate relationship between Southern blacks and whites—a doomed symbiosis that slowly poisons both partners.

"Everybody's racist, black and white," one Mississippi nonagenarian told the New York Times. I'm not sure I believe that, but once I believed it enough to write that it was every American's civic duty to conceive at least one interracial child—the only long-term cure for our terrible disease. My mother was afraid the Klan would make me pay for that one.

And yet a new study finds that 40 percent of Americans have "dated" outside their racial group, a statistic that would have landed like a nuclear missile in Monroe. The old dragons are asleep now; for most of them it's a deep sleep, but never mistake it for death.

Who's Your Daddy?

FATHERS OF US ALL

On T-shirts and bumper stickers you don't see if you live in a gated golf community, the slogan under the Confederate battle flag is "Heritage, not hate." It's a slogan I've been willing to accept, provisionally. The crusade against the Stars and Bars is one of the unexamined excesses of the politically correct. There's too little to be gained, in my opinion, by legislating shame and forcing people to repudiate their history. It was by shaming Germany after World War I that the Allies made Adolf Hitler possible.

If you enjoy political moralizing, take a hard look at the English. They made porters and houseboys out of half the nonwhite peoples of the earth. They made sullen vassals of my Scots ancestors and my Welsh ancestors too. They hanged Nathan Hale and burned Washington, D.C.; they hanged the poor for stealing pennies, as Charles Dickens was one of the first to protest. They created and perpetuate one of the most repugnant caste systems the world has ever seen.

As a Scottish American, I see precious little in their history of which they deserve to be proud. But now that they're a feeble and helpless old nation, I don't advocate ripping down the Union Jack. You have to leave people some self-respect.

A symbol like a flag can be allowed to mean different things to different people. But whenever I get too smug about my logic, along comes another pack of Neanderthals, and I have to eat my battle flag with a double order of crow. They were right down the road this time, at Randolph Community College in Archdale, North Carolina. A history course titled "North Carolina's Role in the War for Southern Independence" (note the nuanced language) was suspended after the *Greensboro News and Record* reported that its instructors had resurrected the notorious Happy Slave Dance.

The instructors, members of Lt. F. C. Frazier Camp 668 of the Sons of Confederate Veterans, were alleged to be teaching that 70 percent of former slaves had been "satisfied" with their lives before emancipation.

"These people loved the South," according to instructor Herman White, an Archdale minister. "They weren't looking for some Yankees to come down and save them."

And the chase was on. The wire services picked up the story, the NAACP expressed outrage, the state advisory committee to the U.S. Commission on Civil Rights requested a formal inquiry, and the beleaguered president of Randolph Community College canceled the Sons' last class. Tony Horwitz, author of the best-selling *Confederates in the Attic*, offered his opinion that "This is happening somewhere in the South on almost a weekly basis."

The Sons of Confederate Veterans, of course, deny any bigotry or distortion. Here was another curious case of dueling interpretations. The Archdale Confederates seem to base their "happy slave" statistics on a series of interviews with former slaves that were conducted by the Federal Writers' Project in the 1920s and 1930s.

These same interviews, recently published as *Remembering Slavery* by the New Press, were discussed by Yale historian Edmund S. Morgan in the *New York Review of Books*. "What stands out in all these interviews in grim monotony," Morgan writes, "is the unrelenting dominance of masters, maintained by regular whipping and torture, sometimes by exemplary murder."

Apparently it took a lot less to keep an African American happy in those days. Morgan quotes one especially appalling reminiscence by an ancient ex-slave: "Many a day my ole mama has stood by an' watched massa beat her chillin 'till dey bled an' she couldn' open her mouf. Dey didn' only beat us, but they useta strap my mama to a bench or a box an' beat her wid a wooden paddle while she was naked."

As much as any lynching or terminal atrocity, these images are so vivid with injustice and sadism that they make forgiveness and reconciliation seem preposterous. Apparently that's the way it looked to Thomas Jefferson: "Ten thousand recollections by the blacks of the injuries they have sustained would produce convulsions which will probably never end but in the extermination of one or the other race," Jefferson wrote in *Notes on the State of Virginia*.

That's also the way it looked to Stokely Carmichael, an American civil rights leader of enormous ability who died last month in Africa, a permanent expatriate because he couldn't convince himself that America's racial scars might be healed. The irony is that Kwame Ture, as he renamed himself, was just as cruelly disappointed in his idealistic dreams of Pan-African unity and socialism.

Jefferson, of course, used his pessimism as a rationale for maintaining slavery. Slavery was a crime so horrendous, a moral violation so unhinging in its consequences that even a mind like Jefferson's could be turned to unreason in its awful shadow. The white media demonized and minimized black leaders like Carmichael, Rap Brown, and Malcolm X because they were militant and unaccommodating. But Rap and Malcolm were the ones I could understand. Do you beg for rights that have been yours legally since 1865? Do you beg them from the descendants of people who strapped your naked grandmother to a bench and beat her with a wooden paddle?

Carmichael's response was the natural response, the psychologically healthy response to the situation in which he found himself as an African American adult in the 1960s. The race war that Jefferson predicted and Carmichael espoused was a "natural" outcome—and African Americans would have suffered a catastrophic setback. Fortunately for black people of the next generation, other leaders like

Martin Luther King and Thurgood Marshall possessed a truly unnatural patience and Christian forbearance.

The black experience in America has provoked many unnatural responses. When the AKA sorority expelled one of their debutantes because she insisted on wearing Rasta braids with her ball gown, black columnist Barry Saunders of Raleigh's *News and Observer* chastised the young ladies—and unleashed an amazing retaliation from middle-class blacks of the AKA persuasion. It included the N-word and an unflattering assessment of Saunders's physiognomy and pigmentation. It was thunderously embarrassing. Race aside, pity the pundit who tries to deal honestly in this minefield of a culture where some people are so politically hypersensitized and others so woefully obtuse.

Journalists, black and white, often feel driven toward the same conclusion that made Thomas Jefferson a hypocrite and Kwame Ture an exile. William Faulkner called slavery America's Original Sin, the one thing that may defeat us after all. Sons of the Confederates and daughters of the AKAs are fatal partners in cluelessness, unable to understand their own behavior or to judge how it might be perceived (the AKAs could say that this is *their* heritage—one hundred years of trying to act as white as they can).

Legal and economic equality won't save America, in the long run, if we become a self-segregated nation pitting one race warped by guilt against another race warped by victimization. In *A Country of Strangers: Blacks and Whites in America,* David K. Shipler argues that this is already the case. As Shipler sees it, the best public policy and the best of private intentions are making no headway against racial polarization.

Maybe there's only one hope, a subversive hope that provokes jeers from both sides of the aisle. It's based on nothing but fact and logic, which rarely get a place at the table when racial matters are discussed.

Years ago, in a whimsical attempt to offend everyone, I wrote that wholesale miscegenation is the only realistic salvation for a racist society. It was the patriotic duty of a concerned citizen, I said, to produce at least one child of mixed race. And in a hundred years no one would remember what David Duke and Kwame Ture were so upset about.

I wasn't actually joking. More like needling, trolling for racist responses. In a radical newsletter I found a blueprint for the same thing—dead serious—proposing a national service commitment to biracial reproduction, along the lines of the military draft. A program for healthy young people who could pass the physical.

Farfetched and offensive? Come on, it's our heritage. Recent DNA tests prove beyond reasonable doubt that Jefferson fathered at least one son by his slave Sally Hemings. A black family in Illinois is seeking similar tests to prove that their ancestor, one West Ford, was George Washington's son by a slave girl named Venus. People far more blood-proud than the Confederate Sons of Archdale are facing up to the likelihood that they have cousins of several colors. The Founding Fathers, it appears, were fathers indeed—fathers to us *all.*

As a professor of mine once demonstrated in a sociology class, it's a rare American who can identify four generations of his ancestors, far less color them accurately. We're not what we claim to be, and we never were. Instead of asking, "Can blacks and whites ever live with each other?" we should have been asking, "What does black or white mean, and why are we stuck with these words?"

The truth—which we've always known—is that race as an exclusive category is pure (or impure) fantasy in America. Black and white are words of pride and racist convenience, not scientific observation. They describe artificial tribes, and they're a sorry legacy from slavery and its hideous offspring, Jim Crow.

"Only a small fraction of the black population in contemporary America is of purely African extraction," confirms historian Joseph Ellis. Facing each other in a recent issue of the *New York Times Book Review* were a drawing of Thurgood Marshall and a photograph of Shelby Steele—"black" men of opposing philosophies—and in each face you could see their European ancestors as clearly as the ones from Africa.

How strange, that to honor one set of ancestors many Americans have to deny or repudiate the other set. In the face of your brother you have to pretend to see a stranger. Sally Hemings was the *half sister* of Jefferson's wife. But slavery bred stranger things yet. The American Constitution said a slave was three-fifths of a human being; it took three generations of mating with whites, Thomas Jefferson calculated, to "clear the blood" in a half-African family. Whites who had been to college gave every evidence that they believed heaven itself was segregated. No doubt some still believe it.

It will take not a color-blind but a thoroughly colored population to put such nightmare nonsense behind us. Before a biracial delegation comes to burn my home, I hope they read black sociologist Orlando Patterson of Harvard, who takes the same tack: "No society ever solved its ethnic problems without intermarriage," writes Dr. Patterson, "and America will be no exception."

Let the slogan be "Do as Jefferson did, not as he said." Let golfer Tiger Woods, the one-man Rainbow Coalition, serve as a racial ideal. Europeans may feel nostalgia for familiar characteristics of their racial type—Irish eyes, the cold-weather rose that blooms in the Celtic cheek—but Asians and Africans will be making the same sacrifice for harmony and social justice.

Though I'm too old and inbred for any sane breeding program— three undistinguished bloodlines gutter out in the same scruffy Highland clan—I'd gladly serve if called upon, just to set an example for reluctant patriots. Crossbreed for Christ. Jump into the melting pot, the gene pool of the only possible future. Last one in is a racist pig.

The Curse of Shoeless Joe

At the end of the twentieth century, the major leagues had been all but abandoned by those who love baseball most. Good poets have written volumes explaining what we loved and why we loved it. Here, it's enough to say that none of it lives in corporate skyboxes or domed stadiums with eighty-dollar seats. Maybe we're fortunate that big-league baseball at the turn of the century is dominated by George Steinbrenner and his New York Yankees. It makes it so easy to say goodbye. But for purists who honor baseball's past because we can't bear to contemplate its future, there's one piece of unfinished business.

Here was the last baseball story of the waning millennium: Pete Rose on the Internet, waging a grassroots campaign to regain his eligibility for the Baseball Hall of Fame. Early e-mail returns looked good for Pete—America has no memory and no great respect for facts, and loves to forgive a hero who hits bottom almost as much as it loves to destroy him when he's riding high.

Rose's fate is a matter of serene indifference to me. The Hall of Fame ain't what it used to be, and the Internet campaign was just another roll of the dice by a compulsive gambler who unquestionably bet on the team he was managing. As a onetime sportswriter who has sniffed him up close, I can affirm that Pete Rose has all the charm and humanity of the swollen rodent he's come to resemble. But let them hold their noses and put Rose in the Hall on his record as a player—as long as Shoeless Joe Jackson goes in first.

This is about justice but it's also a Blue-Gray thing, a chance for the South to reclaim a piece of its pride that hostile Yankees long ago soiled and buried. No player hated the chilly North more than the great Joseph Jefferson Jackson, who hopped a train for the Carolinas every time he got the blues. Is it a coincidence that Kenesaw Mountain Landis, the ruthless commissioner who banned Joe for life (and afterlife), was named after a Civil War battle in which his father lost a leg to a Confederate cannonball?

It's the painful truth that American baseball was a Yankee invention. Historians agree that Southerners learned the game during The War, from Union prisoners who often packed a bat and ball in their field gear. Three decades later, in 1897, just three major league players—out of 168—hailed from as far south as Virginia. Another Southerner, Kentucky's talented George Treadway, had just been hounded out of the National League by Northern racists who thought he looked like a Negro.

Joe Jackson was nine years old, already working in the Brandon cotton mill outside Greenville, South Carolina, already marked as a natural by members of the mill baseball team who watched him on the sandlots. He joined the Brandon team at thirteen, playing with men in their twenties and thirties. At fifteen, converted from a pitcher to an outfielder, he was the star of the mill league and a regional legend. No one ever claimed to have taught Joe Jackson anything. Shoeless Joe with his famous bat, forty-eight-ounce Black Betsy, materialized out of the Carolina cotton fields almost as mysteriously as his ghost stepped out of the Iowa cornfield in the movie fantasy *Field of Dreams*.

In baseball's Golden Age, when the South's morale was still recovering from Appomattox and Reconstruction, Joe Jackson was the most celebrated homegrown hero since Stonewall. Sometimes they called him "Stonewall" or "General," sometimes "the Southern Whirlwind" and "the Carolina Confection." Sportswriters of the day,

Homeric in their aspirations, were in the business of crafting myths. Is it true that Jackson, just to show off, threw a ball from deep center that cleared the grandstand behind home plate? Did Black Betsy launch line drives so savage that infielders ducked them, outfielders froze, fences shattered, and pitchers wet themselves in fear? I'm not sure I believe that Jackson hit a ball to center so hard that it handcuffed Tris Speaker, perhaps the best outfielder ever, and struck him in the neck. But I love to read about it.

In those days every self-respecting scribe practiced doggerel. A scrap that survives attests to Jackson's reputation:

When Jackson steps up to the plate
To hit the horsehide ball
The fielders get so far away
They really look quite small.

But the same writers who made Jackson a folk hero would make him, at other times, a laughingstock. His illiteracy and mill-hand origins made him an easy target. Sportswriters loved to pass on the story—perhaps apocryphal—that Connie Mack's Philadelphia Athletics took the rookie Jackson to an upscale restaurant and tricked him into drinking the finger bowl. When Joe jumped the Athletics and went home to Greenville (twice), homesickness was portrayed as simplemindedness by the Northern press.

Even his signature myth, the source of his nickname, is a gross distortion of the facts. Jackson was never discovered playing barefoot. From the age of thirteen he was supplied with the best spiked shoes the Brandon mill bosses could afford. But one day a pair of new spikes blistered his feet so painfully he couldn't wear any shoes. The manager made his star play anyway, in his stocking feet.

One of baseball's most enduring myths was born. In the biography *Say It Ain't So, Joe* (no heartbroken kid ever said that to Jackson outside the courtroom, either), Donald Gropman labors to set the record straight. He establishes that sportswriters of Joe's day operated with a reckless disregard for facts. They were relatively harmless when they were amusing and edifying the nation's schoolboys. When they covered critical stories like the Black Sox World Series fix of 1919, which destroyed Joe Jackson's life, they could be lethally irresponsible.

In the wake of America's most notorious sports scandal, few writers seemed interested in the guilt or innocence of individual players, or intrigued by the fact of Jackson's outstanding performance in the Series he was accused of tanking for the gamblers. Instead they churned out the predictable cautionary tale, the moral fable of the ignorant hayseed seduced by city slickers, the idol with feet of clay who betrayed the trust of America's youth.

That's the way most Americans still see him. Gropman makes a strong case for Jackson's literal innocence. He documents Joe's attempt to warn White Sox owner Charles Comiskey before the Series, as well as his efforts to return the $5,000 in cash Lefty Williams threw on his bed when the Series was over. Gropman's book claims that the team's lawyer, protecting Comiskey, tricked Jackson into signing a confession he couldn't read.

Eighty years of investigations failed to answer half our questions about the Black Sox. Jackson died, in 1951, maintaining that he did nothing wrong. Among those who believed him were Ted Williams and Bob Feller, who petitioned for his reinstatement. By any reckoning, the case against Jackson was weaker than the case against Pete Rose, or even the case baseball brought against Ty Cobb, the first of "the immortals" inducted into its Hall of Fame. There's a signed letter linking Cobb to a game-fixing conspiracy in 1919, the same year the White Sox threw the Series. But Commissioner Landis exonerated Cobb, an intimate of senators and presidents and the reigning star of the game.

Pitchers who faced Shoeless Joe, including Babe Ruth, testify that Jackson could time and drive a fastball like no man who ever lived. In every other way his timing was tragic. His road to fame and fortune was mined with mean-spirited Yankees; he reached the major leagues when owners were starting to make real money and paying players hardly any—a discrepancy that an army of gamblers and hoodlums was arrayed to exploit. Thanks to Ty Cobb, Joe was never the most successful hitter in the American League, not even the most successful left-handed hitter from the South. Jackson hit an incredible .393 for his first three seasons in the league; Cobb, his country neighbor from across the state line in Royston, Georgia, averaged a supernatural .408 and outhit him every year.

Timing is fate, and fate throws some curve balls that no one can hit. It's nothing to Shoeless Joe, fifty years dead, if a bunch of corporate flunkies decide he's fit for Cooperstown, where a Union general was erroneously credited with inventing baseball. We're fighting this one for pride and sentiment, for our grandfathers who witnessed Jackson's exploits and grew up with his legend.

Once the South had Cobb to be proud of, too, but Al Stump's definitive 1994 biography exposed the "Georgia Peach" as a vicious sociopath who specialized in stolen bases and aggravated assault. Cobb, like Rose, was the best of ballplayers and the worst of men. Kids who begged these pit bulls for an autograph were lucky to walk away with all the fingers on the hand that held the scorecard. The kids always loved Joe Jackson, a gentle man with no children of his own.

The Hall of Fame won't evict the unspeakable Cobb, who beat his own son with a bullwhip for flunking out of college; eventually it will forgive the unmentionable Rose. But no one south of Baltimore should ever cast a vote for Rose unless the resurrection of Shoeless Joe is part of the deal. It's the right thing to do. If we do it now, maybe the grieving old gods of baseball will see fit to lift this curse they've laid upon the game.

Sacred Art, Southern Fried

HARLOTS AND HELLFIRE

It's not well known that I was once, for a very short run, an actual salaried art critic for a large northern newspaper. But it's my reputation as an independent theologian that best qualifies me to comment on the paintings of the late Reverend McKendree Long. As a lapsed Unitarian I fall at the opposite end of the theological spectrum from Reverend Long. Maybe the only thing we had in common was a taste for the sort of woman the tabloids call "statuesque." Surely I'd be among the lost souls he sent hurtling into the Lake of Fire, in their bathing suits or less. Members of my family have even been guilty of that heresy know as Universalism, the bland and beautiful belief that everyone is saved whether they like it or not—"the final harmony of all souls with God"—and that even if you ended up in hell somehow it was only temporary. It just meant that you and God needed to get a few things straight between you. I myself once wrote, in an art review, "I've never been able to follow the notion of God's plan much beyond the boundaries of the human ego."

I suppose I'd be a secular humanist, if I had a little more faith in humans. I'm profoundly uncomfortable with some of the images in Long's paintings, of Christ with a sword or a bloody sickle, of God orchestrating colossal slaughters and mass extinctions of human and animal life, toward what end we're not really sure, except to confirm to individuals like McKendree Long that they were right all along— that God is as uncompromising and unforgiving as the face they see in the mirror every morning. When it comes to scripture, I line up with the British writer Zadie Smith, who declares in her novel *White Teeth*, "The Book of Revelation is the last stop on the nutso express."

No one knows much about this man John who wrote the book of Revelation on the island of Patmos some time around 100 A.D. Very few scholars still believe that he was John the disciple of Christ. All we know is that he had a lurid and spectacular imagination—like McKendree Long—and that every period of Christian history has produced new and increasingly bizarre interpretations of his prophecy. If I were a biblical scholar, I'd make a study of the vegetation on the isle of Patmos, to see if Patmos grows anything recognizably halluci- nogenic. But in present time John's nutso express is carrying more passengers than ever before, including American fundamentalists who are rooting for World War III in the Middle East because it suits their timetable for Armageddon. A man named Dale Pollett came to my hometown last month with a video-illustrated lecture series, "The Time of the Beast," including a lecture revealing "nine ways to iden- tify the Antichrist—a crystal clear revelation of who the Antichrist IS." First-class passengers on the express also include the Reverend Pat Robertson of Virginia Beach—an educated, gentleman evangelist like McKendree Long—whose book *The End of the Age* prophesied that Christ would return in the year 2000 in a spaceship, a "jew- eled cube" measuring fourteen hundred miles on each side. Reverend Robertson also ran for president in 1988 and won more delegates at the Republican Convention than anyone except George H. W. Bush and Bob Dole.

Speaking of politics—the work of McKendree Long reminds us that it's profoundly important to keep church and state separate, as nearly all the Founding Fathers, mostly deists, Unitarians, or agnos- tics and none of them fundamentalists, insisted from the start. If you believe you're doing exactly what God demands, as Pat Robertson does, why should you care what anyone else thinks? Pat knows what to do with God's enemies—with you and me. And Reverend Long's grandson recalls that "Whatever disagreed with him at the moment went into the picture." That is, into the Lake of Fire or the Bottomless Pit. From Long we got these wonderful paintings—congratulations to the collectors and art historians who, unlike his family, recognized how really singular they are—but imagine what secular humanists would get from President Robertson if he truly believed the Antichrist was on the march.

When you look at the lineup of great souls headed for the Lake of Fire, you see immediately what the reverend has in mind. Damn Bacon, damn Voltaire, damn Darwin and Huxley and Einstein and Freud—Long is throwing out the Age of Reason, the Enlightenment, the scientific revolution, virtually every step forward in human comprehension since the Dark Ages. (After savoring some of his heavy-breathing "Lady in Red" paintings, I thought Reverend Long should have booked a few hours of Sigmund Freud's professional services before he pitched Dr. Freud into the flames.) What he's really saying is that nothing worth reading has been written since John ate those mushrooms on Patmos in 95 A.D. Yet Reverend Long loved to read Robert Browning.

In this exhibition alone (North Carolina Museum of Art, 2002), with his letters and poetry to cross-reference, we can begin to understand how Long's personal torments might have led him to certain theological extremes. Think of Jimmy Swaggart, another multitalented evangelist who sublimated sex—inadequately as I recall—on a keyboard instead of a canvas. But how did this revolt against reason and tolerance come to so afflict the South that to some outlanders it still appears as H. L. Mencken described it, "a cesspool of Baptists, a miasma of Methodism, snake charmers and syphilitic evangelists"?

There's a book by Christine Heyrman, *Southern Cross*, that contradicts the impression that the South has always been this way. "Evangelism came late to the American South," Heyrman writes, "as an exotic import rather than an indigenous development." She portrays the South of the eighteenth century as the homeland of easygoing

Anglicans, doubters, deists, and independent, contentious freethinkers epitomized by Thomas Jefferson, regarded by early fundamentalists as the Antichrist himself. When the Church of England all but abandoned America after the revolution, migrating Scots-Irish and Germans brought hellfire evangelism south along the Appalachians. But it took more than a century of struggle, and ample ridicule, before evangelicals achieved the dominance that Mencken deplored.

"Take care for the Baptists for they will not rest till they dip you," one Virginia Episcopalian warned his neighbor. In 1776 evangelicals claimed just 10 percent of church membership in the South; by the War of 1812 they still claimed less than 20 percent. North Carolina was one of the first places where exotic theology appeared to thrive. Heyrman describes it in 1785 as "a place in the South akin to what Rhode Island had been earlier in New England—a remote exile for those whose religious eccentricities embarrassed more sober Christians."

Baptists and Methodists adapted and gained strength, according to Heyrman, by backing away from what we might now see as their strengths, their early opposition to slavery and their concern for the poor and for the rights of women. But as late as 1822, the great Thomas Jefferson felt so confident of their final failure—and of the rational potential of his countrymen—he committed a piece of prophecy more doomed and naïve than the worst of Pat Robertson, Mckendree Long, or John of Patmos.

"I trust," said Jefferson, "that there is not a Young Man now living in the United States who will not die a Unitarian."

Mencken and Me

INDISCREET CHARMS OF THE BOURGEOISIE

According to legend, Alexander the Great slept every night of his short life with two things under his pillow—his knife and his copy of *The Iliad*. As a boy of fourteen, already identified as a troubled adolescent, I slept with a baseball under my pillow—a ball autographed by major league slugger Del Ennis (which I imagined was much coveted)—and beside my pillow, or never farther than my bedside table, a copy of the yellow *Vintage Mencken* published in 1955, edited by Alistair Cooke. Our respective choices explain in part why Alexander conquered Asia and I became an English major and an essayist. God knows H. L. Mencken was belligerent, even warlike in his popular persona, but there are those of us who know, almost from infancy, that our anger will be expressed with the pen, not the sword; we sense also that there is something appalling about bloody Achilles, the irresistible prima donna, sulking in his tent.

What is it that brings a boy—or a man or, more rarely, a woman—to find comfort in the verbal extravagance and exuberant prejudice of Henry Mencken? In this age of political correctness and elaborate, infuriating systems of rhetorical taboos, it's amusing to see each wave of protest against Mencken's defenseless bones, as women, blacks,

Jews, Muslims, most ethnic groups rediscover that at some point he disparaged them and called them names that have long since become capital crimes in the media and in the academy. Yet it was my own tribe, the rural Anglo-Saxon, that he despised most venomously and to whom, in his most spirited moments, he scarcely granted full membership in the human race. There's a classic passage in *Happy Days,* classic for the way it unites the redneck and the African American, cringing together under Mencken's lash:

> a great many anthropoid blacks from the South have come to town since the city dole began to rise above what they could hope to earn at home, and soon or late some effort may be made to chase them back. But if that time ever comes the uprising will probably be led, not by native Baltimoreans, but by the Anglo-Saxon baboons from the West Virginia mountains who have flocked in for the same reason, and are now competing with the blacks for the poorer sort of jobs.

Isn't that refreshing? My people, the mountain baboons. The truth is that Mencken, in his beleaguered German American chauvinism, so loathed the Anglo-Saxons on both sides of the Atlantic that he might have exulted to see our Motherland overrun by the Kaiser—or conceivably, at one point, by the Führer—and Buckingham Palace converted to a biergarten and hofbrauhaus. But somehow this bigotry didn't trouble me, even though my grandfather's dining room was decorated with portraits of the six queens of England, with Victoria in the place of honor over the sideboard and Bloody Mary scowling in the darkest corner. Apparently it didn't trouble my grandfather either, because he was the one who presented me with my *Vintage Mencken.* Middle-class Anglo-Saxons, notoriously smug, aren't so quick to take offense at mere verbal assaults and impertinences. There was a time—Mencken's time, which may have ended with the Great Depression—when outrageous exchanges between clever people were considered good sport, not grounds for public demonstrations and emergency legislation.

If there's one pejorative that might describe my kind and excellent grandfather, that word is *complacent*. Like Mencken, who was eight years older, he was the pampered first son of a successful businessman, a son of whom much was expected as long as it ended in the family business. The more I read about Mencken, the less difference I see between the German and English legacies, or between urban and rural—my family was as dyed-in-the-wool small town as the Menckens were urban—and the more I sense an almost identical class heritage. The American bourgeoisie that developed between the Civil War and the First World War, as opposed to the plutocracy of robber barons, was characterized by self-reliance, scrupulous honesty, supernatural self-confidence—which my father inherited from his father and I have somehow misplaced—and an amiable contempt for individuals with different experiences and beliefs.

If I had to make one negative assertion about Mencken's personality, one I think I could defend, it's that he was somewhat deficient in empathy. He didn't come to grips with the Great Depression because—unlike Prohibition—it had a minimal impact on him personally. His cavalier endorsement of wholesale capital punishment in *Minority Report*—"If we had 2000 executions a year in the United States instead of 130, there would be an immense improvement"—is for me one of the least appetizing of his contrarian performances. It shows not only a limited ability to empathize with the accused—as if criminals and columnists come from different galaxies—but an uncharacteristic and contradictory impulse to place great faith in the judgment of juries and district attorneys. And yet he carried on an extensive correspondence with prisoners; this is not the easiest man to pigeonhole.

If Mencken failed to understand that people suffered real pain from his wrathful outbursts, it was because he himself had a hide as thick as *Tyrannosaurus rex*. This was an advantage typical of his class and his generation, as I remember them. My grandfather, who read *The Smart Set* in college and bequeathed Mencken to his sons and grandsons, would sit enthroned on his front porch under the trumpet vine, smoking a cigar, and deliver a running, often scathing and hilarious commentary on every unfortunate soul who passed by, on foot or by automobile. He called them by affectionate but condescending contractions of their surnames, like "old Bergie" (superintendent of schools Carl Bergerson) and "poor Farny" (Harold Farnsworth). As in "there goes poor Farny in that rustbucket Packard he couldn't trade for a pony."

He showed no anger, ever, and no mercy. In his time my father was even less charitable. It was this easy contempt that I inherited, that I came in time to be ashamed of, and of which I have long struggled to cure myself.

No one can ever compete with Mencken as a target for other people's invective. But with a thick hide of my own I've weathered tidal waves of abuse from my fellow Tar Heels, unleashed in equal volumes by Dixiecrat reactionaries who call themselves Republicans—shaming the party of Lincoln and Theodore Roosevelt my family followed faithfully for a hundred years—and suede-glove fascists of the PC Left who take violent exception to my careless terms of discourse. But the only criticism that ever held my attention was a satirical song composed by an outlaw songwriter who called himself the Reverend Billy C. Wirtz, a working-class troubadour who sported tattoos on every inch of skin between his navel and his Adam's apple. In his song, this Bertolt Brecht of the Bible Belt dismissed me as "the intellectual guru of the North Raleigh yuppies." It stung me because I always thought of myself as the champion of the underdog and, more like Mencken, the implacable enemy of the country club, gated-community crowd that had only recently been designated "yuppies" in the national media.

I don't think the Reverend Wirtz was precisely on target, because I don't think he'd ever met enough yuppies to understand what makes them tick. But with the bloodhound's nose of the intuitive plebeian, he had sniffed out the middle-class privilege that often produces a belligerent enemy of middle-class beliefs. If you feel entitled, you feel entitled to protest. You don't sneer at the status quo if you're struggling and scheming to use it to your advantage, if your goal is to find a safe place for yourself within that same status quo.

Scorn is expensive. Perhaps it takes at least two generations of successful businessmen to create a great cynic like Henry Mencken. Though I may be more of a democrat, with a small *d*, than Mencken, I think his contempt for democracy was entirely justified. Democracy honors the wisdom of the herd, and the herd has never proven itself worthy of that honor, never to the slightest degree. But to the Reverend Billy C. Wirtzes of the world, it's democracy, not property, that separates them from the serfs in Gogol's *Dead Souls* who are reduced to advocating their own floggings for the greater good of Russia—a level of "slave morality" even lower than those Mencken castigated.

It's a class thing, like so many of the most significant distinctions in this country where we refuse to talk about class. It takes a certain kind of family to incubate a critic, a columnist, a cynic, an iconoclast—someone with the serene self-confidence to assert in public that he is right and the herd, however vast or menacing, is not only wrong but ridiculous. I know what kind of family it takes because I grew up in one, and so, I submit, did Mencken. His grandfather, Burkhardt Mencken, he remembered as "generally confident and even somewhat cocky," and biographer Fred Hobson adds that Burkhardt showed "an independent spirit from the beginning, as well as a certain defiance of civil authority."

The expression on the face of his father, August Mencken, in a photograph that Mencken himself took in 1895—that's my grandfather's expression to the finest shading: faintly amused, just slightly combative, thoughtful but supremely self-satisfied, sure of his place in the world. The cigar and vest and watch chain are identical too, though I can't remember my grandfather in a derby. The details of Mencken's life in his father's home—the summer vacations and family holidays, the cult of baseball, the way neighbors and even police looked indulgently upon the misdemeanors of the children of respectable families, the piano-centered parlor, the cultural assumptions that were not always of the highest order but not known to be less—these discreet charms of the bourgeoisie that I knew in my own childhood almost bring me to nostalgic tears.

Freethinkers long before they emigrated from Yorkshire, my father's family was not in any serious sense religious. But my brother and I—exactly like Mencken and his brother Charlie—were sent to Methodist Sunday school to acquire some acquaintance with the Christian faith, in case we should ever need it. We know how savagely Mencken turned on the Methodists. As for me, I was no less precocious or obnoxious than the adolescent Jesus disputing his elders in the temple. I asked the hardest questions of the dumbest teachers—for instance, "Why should I love my enemies if God sends his to hell?"—and was widely identified as God's enemy before I was nine years old.

None of which troubled my father to any noticeable degree. He himself grew up privileged in the twenties, before the market crash and the Great Depression knocked some of the stuffing out of the middle class, and his self-regard was legendary. He once told us—after several martinis, to be quite fair—that there were four or five men in the world, no more, who clearly surpassed him in intellectual agility. My brother, himself no slacker in the satirical arts, began to introduce Dad to his friends as the Sixth Smartest Man in the World, or Number Six or Big Six, like Christy Mathewson. Though I am, like Mencken, the eldest son of an eldest son of an only son, and have spent most of my adult life dispensing opinions for a living, I do not exaggerate if I claim to be the most modest and least opinionated male my family has produced since the Civil War.

I knew these Menckens the first time I encountered them, felt the pull of class consanguinity right down to my DNA. Mencken himself never questioned his family's influence on his own unique development. "How did I get my slant on life? Heredity," he told an interviewer in 1926. "My ancestors for three hundred years back were all bad citizens. . . . They were always against what the rest were for. . . . I was prejudiced when I came into the world."

The rock-solid middle-class family that kept him, in his words, "fat, saucy and contented," was paradoxically the perfect nest for a nestling who set himself the task of dismantling Middle America brick by brick. At the same time, it provided him with a character-forming mythology, a middle-class ideal that exalted respectable people—"decent" was a word Mencken used—people who pay their debts, live within their means, answer to no one. In his time, people who paid cash. My grandfather bought his automobiles with rolls of hundred-dollar bills. This ideal included the code of the gentleman: that the weak are not to be bullied and exploited, that other people are not stepping stones to goals, that truth is never the product of consensus, that money is a means not an end, that honor and reputation are more important than wealth and preference.

I grew up marinated in this code; so did Mencken. For business-men like his father and my grandfathers there was no conflict be-tween the code of the gentleman and the law of the marketplace; in fact they were viewed as a seamless fit. Judge for yourself how times and men and marketplaces have changed.

But Henry Mencken was a man of books, not of business. The middle class is proverbially boring, and in its heyday its talented, em-powered sons and daughters would tend to romanticize the work-ing class, and become Marxists, or romanticize the upper classes and aspire, at least, to become mandarins. Mencken, who was more of a romantic than he'd ever admit, leaned toward the second, the man-darin error. He demonized the Puritans as the poison in America's bloodstream and so offered his allegiance to their nemeses, the Cava-liers—an aristocracy of discriminating gentlemen that he and few others could discern among the cleft-chinned louts in riding breeches chasing foxes.

Though I briefly suffered from a similar delusion—it may be en-demic to hyperimaginative children of the stolid bourgeoisie—it was never one of the sturdier planks in Mencken's platform. (Mencken claimed German nobility on some collateral branch of his family tree; the only royalty in my family tree was Uncle Johnny Briar, self-styled "the Mum King," the Yorkshire greenhouseman who supplied the chrysanthemums for Queen Elizabeth's coronation in 1953.)

To me there was always something fishy about Mencken's veneration of James Branch Cabell. If anything can be said in defense of democracy, let's say that there's more promise in trying to educate a drooling mob—if a society actually wishes to educate it—than in waiting a thousand years for a dynasty of syphilitic halfwits to produce a philosopher king, or for some blue-blood rabble of human foxhounds to produce, in Mencken's words, "a few first-rate men." Mencken berates America for its failure to produce an adequate aristocracy, and its failure to preserve what it had long enough to save us from the Puritan baboons. But England's whey-brained House of Windsor and its doddering House of Lords are painful examples of what happens when an aristocracy wears out its welcome.

It's ironic that Mencken, middle class to the bone, sworn exterminator of the genteel pretensions of most of his countrymen, romanticized some long-lost class of enlightened squires writing learned treatises in paneled libraries in the lulls between Europe's wars. Because he himself was the representative, the strutting epitome of a class that promised civilization so much more.

We're used to Mencken's portraits, often caustic or condescending, of his famous friends. But Theodore Dreiser's droll description of Mencken the Boy Wonder is a priceless piece of prose that turns the tables, and adds immeasurably to our comprehension of the Mencken phenomenon:

> There appeared in my office a taut, ruddy, blue-eyed, snub-nosed youth of twenty-eight or nine whose brisk gait and ingratiating smile proved to me at once enormously intriguing and amusing. More than anything else he reminded me of a spoiled and petted and possibly over-financed brewer's or wholesale grocer's son who was out for a lark. With the sang-froid of a Caesar or a Napoleon he made himself comfortable in a large and impressive chair. . . .

There he is to the life—the burgher prince. Do we ever see him more clearly? The bright-eyed, bushy-tailed standard-bearer of an unbowed, unbenighted bourgeoisie that was one of the finest flowers of this republic—the first middle class in history that rose up entirely unburdened by thousands of years of feudalism and the humiliations of caste. With its gene pool replenished by the nineteenth-century immigrants, with a fresh mix of bloodstreams that had never before been combined (Mencken had an Anglo grandmother), America boasted, for a few fleeting, splendid decades, a new class that could think for itself and speak for itself, with or without the leadership of the fading aristocracy or the elusive intelligentsia that never lived up to Mencken's expectations.

When Mencken talks about "a new aristocracy" of artists and writers, it sounds like a pipe dream to me. Yet he himself was living proof of something more vital and more unique. People who didn't come from this class, who haven't studied its history and literature with full comprehension, don't quite know how to take Henry Mencken.

In their incomprehension, readers tend to turn him to every purpose, as Christians turn their Jesus Christ. Conservatives celebrate his hatred for democracy, and for FDR and the New Deal, and conveniently forget that he held the whole chorus line of Republican presidents, from Teddy Roosevelt through Herbert Hoover, in similar contempt (and according to Fred Hobson, actually voted for FDR in 1944 because he saw so little in Dewey). It's dishonest to overlook two Mencken quotations of great current interest, to wit:

> Perhaps the most revolting character that the United States ever produced was the Christian businessman.

And

> In this world of sin and sorrow there is always something to be thankful for; as for me, I rejoice that I am not a Republican.

Those who draft him for a conservative icon deceive themselves grossly if they doubt that he'd have made a roaring satirical bonfire of Ronnie Reagan and Maggie Thatcher—and, of course, cheerfully tossed Jesse Jackson and Ralph Nader into the flames. Victim-group liberals scandalized by his insensitive language choose to forget that he was a powerful enemy to the racists and lynchers of his day, and the first influential critic and editor to promote the work of black writers and of many, many women.

Like every authentic freethinker, Mencken was both a radical and a reactionary, depending on the case at hand. I think of my father when his fellow Republicans called him a liberal because he was soft on—well, fill in the blank. "I'm not a liberal," he said, "I'm a logical—and you're not." If you force me to squeeze myself into some of those meaningless labels that tyrannize the slack-jawed media, I say I'm a social liberal, an economic moderate—anyplace further to the left and my Republican and Scottish ancestors would rise swarming from their graves—and a psychological reactionary.

It's impossible to reconcile the Promethean Mencken, the Enlightenment philosophe, with Mencken the mossback misanthrope; you'll split your head trying. But the key to Mencken, I believe—and the key psychological bridge between the class he came from and the aristocracy he overrated—is what Ford Madox Ford, in *Parade's End*, calls "the passionate Tory sense of freedom."

The first time I read that phrase, I experienced the same frisson of recognition that hit me when I read about Mencken's family. I love Grandpa Burkhardt Mencken for his "defiance of civil authority." Though both my father and grandfather were trained in the law, friends from more timid families—like my wife—were always scandalized to learn that I obey only the laws I agree with, along with a few I'm afraid to break.

I know I've always had that extreme, almost irrational sense of personal freedom—of course Mencken had it—but where did it come from? It's a legacy, I believe, from the first middle class that was ever free enough—personally, politically, historically—free and fearless enough to develop a libertarian obsession once unique to the landed gentry, to the blooded Tory.

For a man of independent philosophy there is nothing on earth more repugnant than the notion that his life is controlled, or in any way altered, by the whims of the mob. It provokes existential claustrophobia. It's the classic Nietzschean dilemma, stated best by William Blake—"one law for the lion and the ox." But democracy settles for mediocrity, muddle, even farce to avoid the body count that mounts when willful giants collide.

There was a wonderful quote at the end of a recent *New York Times* obituary for the great harmonica virtuoso Larry Adler, who was blacklisted and in effect banished from America in 1952 by the witch-hunters of the House Un-American Activities Committee. "Resist the pressure to conform," said Adler, reflecting on fifty years of exile in London. "Better to be a lonely individualist than a contented conformist."

Adler was also born and raised in Baltimore, back in the days of H. L. Mencken and Babe Ruth, when there must have been a powerful strain of infectious freedom loose in this city. "The passionate Tory sense of freedom" can take you left or right, depending on your other passions and the natural shape of your mind. It made Mencken a contrarian, a libertarian, and a political lone wolf. Do you have any idea how much courage—and how much arrogance—it took for a 35-year-old newspaperman to sit in Baltimore and cheer for Germany in World War I, a minority of one flying in the teeth of one of the most poisonous spasms of jingoism America ever produced? It's a true miracle he wasn't lynched.

Risk life, limb, and livelihood for a principle, for a prejudice? It's impossible to place Mencken in a context the twenty-first century can understand, in our cultural cul-de-sac where the eloquent knights-errant of the editorial pages have been replaced by TV "news" shows geared to the depth and dignity of professional wrestling—tag teams of predictable hacks and eunuchs squealing in ersatz fury and quacking partisan platitudes. Seating Mencken on *Crossfire* would be like releasing a wolverine among neutered cats.

In the years since Mencken's death, "What would Mencken say now?" is a game his spiritual descendants play all too often, as Charles Fecher observed in his fine book on Mencken's thought. But the best way to locate Mencken politically is to think of him as an enemy of repression in all its forms, or at least in every form he was capable of recognizing. He cast himself as civilization's Avenging Angel, raining the holy fire of his contempt on every mythology that threatened personal freedom—most particularly Mencken's personal freedoms. In his eyes, those false mythologies included mainstream religion, Main Street morality, bloody-flag patriotism, civic boosterism, the genteel philosophies of Emersonian academics, and the saccharine optimism of bad poets.

The Frankenstein monster Mencken patched together from all these mind-enslaving myths was his bête noire the plutocracy, "the booboisie," the craven, mob-minded majority of his own comfortable class who scorned the light he offered them. The affluent imbeciles, the subclass my daughter—who loves alliteration as much her father—identified in her freshman year at the University of North Carolina as "rich rednecks from Rocky Mount."

The plutocracy: this critical mass of negative intellect, this black hole of inertia, this obese and decomposing albatross strung around the nation's neck. Capitalism's soft underbelly, its dirty secret: prosperity can make us kings or it can make us grasping, groveling slaves. Henry Mencken arrived on the scene at the moment of truth, when America's Great Experiment might have gone either way. The brain-dead plutocracy was his dragon to slay, his windmill to tilt at, his personal version of Don Quixote's quest.

We know that he never dispatched the dragon. The pen may be mightier than the sword, but we live now in a fallen republic where it proved to be weaker than the dollar. There was once a confident, irresistible middle class, a formidable yeomanry of farmers and small businessman that prosperity created and that not even the great wars and the Great Depression could thoroughly destroy. But something destroyed it, and along with it much of this country's potential to live up to its fanfare and its own best instincts.

Mencken warned us in 1944 that "Americans were living in a totalitarian state without knowing it." He meant that Roosevelt was now a king who could do as he wished with America. But in a few months Roosevelt was dead and the war was over. The United States, its male population thinned out considerably by the technological wonders of modern warfare, nevertheless found enough breeding pairs for a stupendous baby boom and supposedly rode a huge new wave of prosperity and optimism into the second half of the twentieth century.

Just how much that optimism had to do with freedom we can imagine from the McCarthy witch hunts, the blacklists, the Red-haunted congressmen scared to death of Larry Adler and his socialist harmonica. But Mencken, incapacitated by his stroke in 1948, was absent from the gallery just when his wit and corrosive contempt might have shamed a few politicians and saved the country serious embarrassment.

H. L. Mencken has not been replaced. For reasons more complex than the fact that he was an American original, no one ever claimed his critical role as our culture's snarling watchdog. A few of us have tried to bear witness in a fashion we hope he would have endorsed. But there have been vertiginous changes since 1948, changes defying the usual rationalizations that the ascent of man is a slow one, at best, and that history runs in cycles. In my own short time, spanning most of those six decades since Mencken warned us about American totalitarianism, I've seen the national mythology change radically and forever.

I need to define "mythology" as I use it, and explain why I choose it over more popular but irritating academic terms like "template" and "paradigm shift." What I mean by "mythology" is the whole narrative structure that animates a particular society, the story line that no one can avoid, that most people accept without question, and without which its whole culture would be incomprehensible. Mencken raged against the loathsome Puritan/Calvinist myth that God is a prig and a bully who is always watching us and is never amused. That was the story, he believed, behind the Protestants' grave failures of humor, imagination, tolerance, and taste. And these failures explained their resistance to anything Mencken defined as a free and civilized society.

But bluestockings, Prohibitionists, book burners, and Methodist prudes are no longer major players in the American drama; FDR in his prime was a cute Dutch Uncle compared with the forces that emerged to fill the vacuum when he died. The last time Mencken looked around with all his own powers intact, conservatives were still agonizing over the power of the state and liberals were striving to empower the working man. Today the working man has disappeared from America's mythology, if not from its farms and cities. Today no one complains about the power of the government except exotic entertainers like Rush Limbaugh and Gordon Liddy, on radio stations wholly owned by media conglomerates owned in turn by multinational corporations more powerful than our government or any government.

What, exactly, changed our script so drastically that Mencken and Samuel Clemens, who knew all our dirty tricks and darkest secrets, would scarcely recognize us now?

It's illuminating to pick up the story of America where Mencken most reluctantly left it in 1948—to extend the trajectory of a few of his major concerns. I don't boast much about my credentials for this line of work. When I confess that I was once a television critic, and also a writer of television programs, I confess it much the way an old German confesses that he was an SS officer—reluctantly, with abject assurances of my remorse and my efforts to atone for my crimes. I won't argue with you about the toxic impact of this technology. There are many depressing studies on the way television affects a child's emotional development, his attention span, his test scores. TV seems to shrink a child's conscience and expand his capacity for violence. There's no doubt in my mind that anyone who logs the national average of six or seven hours a day has suffered so much cerebral atrophy, if not actual brain damage, that no cautious society would allow him to vote, or to breed.

Epidemics of depression and obesity have both been traced to America's perverted passion for electronic information, a mere prelude to dire genetic consequences for a species of creatures who now, with computers added to their menu, routinely stare at glowing rectangles up to fifteen hours a day. In Mencken's generation of writers, only E. B. White offered anything oracular on the effects of television; his line, in hindsight, is chilling: "I'm sure our society will rise or fall on this invention."

White wrote that in 1938. If you want to find dire prophecies that have been fulfilled and exceeded, read or shock yourself by reread-ing Neil Postman's *Amusing Ourselves to Death* or Jerry Mander's *Four Arguments for the Elimination of Television*. But I'll try to limit myself to the issues Mencken addressed most urgently: the vitality and so-cial relevance of literature and the arts and, above all, the survival of our civil and personal liberties, of the vaunted passion for freedom every American demagogue trumpets and every generation sells off cheaper than the one before.

What has television to do with freedom? Advertising was begin-ning to spread like kudzu back in the nineteenth century; it was sub-ject to satire before Mencken was born. But when a careless Con-gress decided to allow unlimited commercial exploitation of the new technology and what were once designated as the people's airwaves, it gave corporate America an advertising tool so powerful, a Trojan Horse so irresistible that a critical balance of power—between cul-ture and commerce, between conscience and concupiscence—was upset for all time. TV was too potent, our resistance too feeble. Ide-alists determined to educate the masses were eclipsed by predators determined to exploit them for profit, and the slow learning curve of centuries was overturned. Not long ago I attended one of those do-it-yourself New Age weddings; the bride's homespun wedding vows mentioned both the TV and the computer—I swear to God.

Just as any American who questioned the perfection of capital-ism was once called a communist, anyone who questions the perfect wisdom of the new technology is called, with equal animus, a Lud-dite. By this yardstick I am an incorrigible Luddite, and proud of it. No one knew exactly what these gadgets could do to us. There was no conspiracy per se. But the material fantasies of corporate advertis-ing, crafted to fleece herd slaves and yokels, have in that short wired space of fifty years become the very air we breathe.

Nearly everything in our lives is now shaped by and for market-ing—even literature. The marginally literate infer, from the amount of attention they receive, that novels are the dominant literary life form. Yet if you want to read the best work American writers produce, you'll find it in short stories, poetry, perhaps even essays. Novels, most of them obese, clunky, and overplotted, baited with soap opera and spurious sex, are simply easier to market and sell for thirty dollars. The novel as pure marketing device, recently introduced by the Italian jeweler Bulgari and the British literary prostitute Fay Weldon, is a thing too vile for Mencken to have imagined in his wildest dreams. But it was the next logical step for a TV culture that erased those obsolete distinctions between creative content and commercial message.

The hypnotic force of electronic advertising actually turned popular culture on its head. Once it was the study of a people's free choices, from an unlimited menu of possibilities; now it's a cynical lab science for marketing technicians, who test their baby-food formulas on a captive population. Everything the labs are feeding us was concocted for the sole purpose of creating more docile, more perfect consumers and corporate employees. Not long ago some academic annoyed me with what sounded like reverence for popular culture, and I replied that popular culture has become an oxymoron.

Freedom-lovers experience spoon-fed culture as oxygen deprivation, as the slow suffocation of free choice and free speech by a plutocracy of fewer and fewer, bigger and bigger corporate entities. Capitalism—once so anarchic in the United States, so pluralistic—is not to blame so much as giantism and the dark arts of techno-hypnosis these giants employ. When it still shared the power with unions and farmers, corporate America spoke in a voice that was often flattering and persuasive. Now that the last pockets of resistance are disappearing, its voice is getting harsh and scornful, impatient. To comprehend the new American mythology, hold your nose and watch one of the new "reality" programs on TV. Here we are, stark naked—contempt for losers, contempt for privacy, dignity, integrity, compassion, any scruple that hobbles the will to prevail. It's the primitive Darwinian proposition, the war of all against all, motivated by petty acquisitiveness—the visceral greed of jackals.

Is this the chosen mythology—the pathology—of big business, business mutated and metastasized beyond remembering its roots in August Mencken's tobacco warehouse, in my grandfather's coal trucks? I can't prove it; I never sat in a corporate boardroom. But as a media critic I knew people like Disney's Michael Eisner back when they were common young weasels in slick suits, long before they were eight-foot-tall tycoons on the cover of Fortune. And what I saw then was not promising.

What I see now is a victorious plutocracy, mind-altering marketing technology delivered into its grateful hands like a genie in a magic lamp, purging its captive population of any lingering idealism or self-respect that might get in the way of perfect, seamless, thoughtless consumption. In the decade of *Survivor, The Weakest Link, Big Brother, Love Cruise,* and *Who Wants to Marry a Millionaire?* the prophet who deserves credit is the late Terry Southern, who wrote *The Magic Christian,* a cult novel of the sixties. Southern's hero, the cynical billionaire Guy Grand, tests the lower limits of human potential with tricks like filling a vat of boiling excrement with thousand-dollar bills. At the time it was satire. Now it's on TV seven nights a week.

Guy Grand, of course, is a hero after Mencken's own heart. America's abject surrender to its basest impulses and most unsavory elements was Mencken's own, dear theme, in another time with other villains. My obvious debt to Mencken made me smile the other day, listening to a tape of myself on public radio. I was responding to a host who said David Broder told her he had the deepest faith in the American people. "Broder may be a great reporter," I replied, "but in my experience anyone who extols the wisdom of the people is trying to get away with something." And a recent newspaper article explained to me why I never quite made it as a Unitarian/Universalist, in spite of generations of family tradition and my great respect for the church's philosophy. A Unitarian minister told the reporter that his denomination took "a very optimistic view of human nature."

So what's the fate, in the long run, of these poor lab rats, the wage slaves and marketing statistics most Americans have become? A few years ago I wrote a column on the phenomenon of *karoshi,* death from overwork, which kills ten thousand Japanese workers every year, not including suicides. At that time the Japanese labored more hours in a week or a year than the workforce of any other industrialized nation, by a considerable margin. In a UN study this summer, American workers passed the Japanese as the most overworked workforce in the world, with an annual average of two thousand man-hours apiece, and less vacation by half than any in Europe. Good jobs are precious; employers say take it or leave it, overtime and all. Unions are in steep decline, costs of living and health care soar. Karoshi looms. It's not surprising that the wisest and second funniest feature in your chain newspaper—after Dave Barry—is Scott Adams's comic strip *Dilbert*, which chronicles the office life of desperate wage slaves in cubicles. A recent sample: "Is there more to life than just working?" Dilbert asks his talking dog, his guru. "Yes," the dog replies, "there's also the complaining about work, the nightly periods of unconsciousness and sweet, sweet death."

It's reported that at least 35 percent of all computerized workers are spied upon, electronically, by their employers. By income and education these are middle-class workers (Dilbert is an engineer), yet they enjoy less autonomy, less flexibility in their working lives than the most miserable serf in tsarist Russia. Big Brother is here, with banners declaring "Labor is life," "Privacy is evil," "Technology is salvation." This Wall Street Big Brother may be exactly what unresisting, slave-minded people deserve, according to the strictest Menckenist. But he's a far cry from what most Americans anticipated, as recently as my youth, farther still from what Adams and Jefferson had in mind.

And what of the nineteenth-century's honorable middle class, the merchants' sons bred to pay cash and spit in the emperor's eye? Bought off, I guess, uprooted and forgotten, their small towns, small farms, small businesses buried under Wal-Marts, agribusiness, strip malls, suburban sprawl, gated subdivisions with rich strangers looking out and poor strangers looking in. And without a proud, entitled middle class, as Stalin understood when he purged the kulaks, you can reduce any society to a herd of tired sheep, at the mercy of the shepherds or the wolves. Without its bourgeois backbone our own democracy, which has had its bright moments, becomes the charade Mencken always said it was.

What of the meritocracy, for whom Mencken, in spite of himself, held out so much hope? A Harvard administrator I know compared the university's matriculating freshmen, the creme de la creme of American secondary schools, to "dazed survivors of some bewildering lifelong boot camp." Their servility, conformity, and lack of curiosity disgusted him. I don't think we should anticipate many Menckens in the twenty-first century.

If he could see us now. Hostile revisionists have argued that many of Mencken's ideas were unoriginal, even pedestrian. But it's unfair to diminish a newsroom philosopher by comparing him to the Schopenhauers and Wittgensteins, who brought rare, hard news from the intellectual battlefront. It was his attitude, more than his intellectual payload, that made Mencken great—his attitude and that high-testosterone, up-against-the-wall prose style we'll never see again. In his prime he was a happy warrior for civilization. But he was a warrior of words, and words, in the current deluge of tainted, meaningless information, have lost their weight and their sting.

There's no denying that America has made great strides toward equality since Henry Mencken left the scene. People who used to enter through the back door are CEOs now, and cabinet secretaries. Women have risen rapidly from kitchens to executive suites—without, however, notably improving the moral tone of the plutocracy, or the way it does business. But Mencken would remind us that equality brings no guarantee of freedom. Not when we're all slaves together—equally—under the same few hundred overseers and the same infernal technologies.